**11 WISE DECISIONS THAT
BRAVE YOUNG MEN MAKE**

CHOOSE GREATNESS

D0188404

GARY CHAPMAN
& CLARENCE SHULER

NORTHFIELD PUBLISHING

CHICAGO

Editorial services and additional content provided by Michael DiMarco at Hungry Planet.

Interior and cover design: Erik M. Peterson
Illustrations of authors by Kelsey Fehlberg
Cover illustration of father and son copyright © 2017 by Grandfailure / iStock (886155936). All rights reserved.

ISBN: 978-0-8024-1867-8

We hope you enjoy this book from Northfield Publishing. Our goal is to provide high-quality, thought-provoking books and products that connect truth to your real needs and challenges. For more information on other books and products that will help you with all your important relationships, go to www.moodypublishers.com or write to:

Northfield Publishing
820 N. LaSalle Boulevard
Chicago, IL 60610

3 5 7 9 10 8 6 4 2

Printed in the United States of America

CHOOSE GREATNESS

*Dedicated to all young men who are
willing to make Brave Decisions*

Contents

Introduction

  As two friends writing a book together, we both grew up in the same state, but we lived in very different worlds. I (Gary) was born of white parents. I (Clarence) was born of black parents. Our worlds intersected when we were young, and neither of us have ever been the same. We have listened to each other, we have learned from each other, and we have enriched each other's lives. To put it another way, our lives are better because of each other.

Even though we came from different backgrounds, much of our lives are the same. Both of us are counselors, authors, and speakers. Each of us is married and has children. We have walked with our children through the teen years. We have traveled the world and our books have been translated into many languages. In short—we have both had a great life. Our definition of a "great life" is taking what you have and using it to enrich the lives of others.

We believe that you can enrich the world. You can make it a better place. Some of you can become great musicians, athletes, educators, physicians, business leaders. You can use those skills to enrich the world. However, you will only reach your full potential if you choose greatness. That is, make wise decisions. Throughout the book we will refer to wise decisions, and what we mean is choosing to be brave by committing to do what is right and best for you, and also for other people in your life.

Our hearts are saddened when we sit in our counseling offices and hear the stories of young adults who made poor decisions when they were teens and are now trying to untangle the webs in which they are trapped. Or, when we visit prisons and talk with young men who are there because they made bad decisions.

We are now looking back on our own lives and realize that many of our most important decisions were made when we were teenagers. As we reflect upon the hundreds of individuals we have counseled through the years, we are both convinced that the decisions that are made between the ages of eleven and sixteen will largely determine the quality of life that a man experiences after he becomes an adult. That is why we are writing this book to young men who are in this most important stage of life.

We want to be honest and say that when we talk about "wise decisions," we are talking about very important decisions. We have discovered through the years that the people who sit in our offices for counseling are mostly people who have been impacted by poor decisions. Their lives have been greatly damaged by those decisions.

We are writing with a deep desire to keep you out of the counselor's office, to keep you out of prison, to help you avoid unnecessary diseases, and to keep you from hurting the people who love you the most and from hurting yourself. In short, we want you to have a great life, and we believe that can only happen if you choose to make wise decisions.

If we could sit down on a park bench or at a coffee shop and listen to your story, we would listen intently because we believe that you are extremely important, and that deep within you is the desire, not only to enjoy life, but also to leave the world a better place than you found it.

We are sure that you have already discovered that the world into which you were born is a harsh world. Nations declare war on each other. And individuals often lash out in anger and hurt each other. The sociologists who have studied American culture have called it the "Argument Culture."[1] For many people, arguing is a way of life. They are constantly trying to convince the other person that "I am right, and you are wrong." If they don't win the argument, they often end up fighting each other.

We are convinced that this is *not* the road to a great life. Too many of our young men die before they reach adulthood, and too many of them are scarred for life by the pain they have experienced. We want to communicate that "There is a better way." We will share intimately from our own life experiences when we were young men. We will also share what we have learned as we have counseled people over the last thirty years.

We will also encourage you to find a trusted adult that you can ask questions of while you go through this book—to get you started we have "Ask Yourself" questions at the end of each chapter.

We hope that you will enjoy what you are about to read, but our deepest desire is that you will join us in making "wise decisions." We will focus on eleven wise decisions that will give you a great life.

GARY CHAPMAN and CLARENCE SHULER

CHOOSE TO SEEK WISDOM
FROM PARENTS OR TRUSTED ADULTS

Life was never meant to be lived alone. As young men, we need the wisdom of our fathers and mothers. Otherwise, we may make decisions based solely upon our feelings rather than upon facts. Or, we may be encouraged to make destructive decisions by evil men who seek to enslave us for their own pleasure. Thousands of young men are led down an addictive pathway by drug dealers and gang leaders who offer fun and excitement, but these promises are never based on truth. Addictions are always destructive.

In the original plan every child would have a father and a mother who would love and support each other, and parent their children with love and wisdom. When this plan is followed, children usually grow up to be responsible, caring adults who work to make the world better. Not only does this probably make instant sense to you, but also there is a ton of research that backs this up, as you will see.

Yet many children have watched their parents divorce. Even good parents who deeply love their children can't always protect them from conflict at home. Dr. William Pollock, a Harvard psychologist, discovered that when the father is no longer in the home, the son often suffers from lack of discipline and supervision, and fails to receive a model of what it means to be a man.[1]

Other children have never known their fathers because their parents never married. Thousands of children grow up in homes without fathers.[2] Many of these children will never know their fathers or experience what it means to be loved by them. According to the National Center for Children in Poverty, young men without fathers are "twice as likely to drop out of school," "twice as likely to end up in jail," and four times as likely to need treatment for emotional and behavioral issues as the young men who have fathers.[3]

Reporting on a major study that looks at children's life outcomes across virtually every neighborhood in this country, *New York Times* columnist David Leonhardt notes that the second most important predictor of life outcomes (after family income) is a neighborhood's share of single-parent families. "Notably, the effect of family structure appears especially large for boys," says Leonhardt.[4]

Children in these single-parent families are typically raised by their mothers, grandmothers, aunts, or sometimes foster parents. This is why we feel so strongly that every young man needs to have either a father, or a substitute father in his life. Someone has said, "Tie a boy to the right man, and he almost never goes wrong." We want you to find the "right man." That is why the title of this chapter is "Seek Wisdom from Parents or a Trusted Adult."

As children, we do not choose our parents. We wish that all children could have a father and mother who love each other and are committed to loving and teaching their children. That is why, as counselors, we have invested our lives in helping couples learn how to love and support each other, and to give their children an example of what a healthy marriage looks like.

When you were a small child your father and mother, or someone who served as your parents, made decisions for you. They determined what you ate and drank. They decided what clothes you would wear. They provided the bed in which you slept. As you got older, they began to let you make some decisions. They asked questions such as, "Would you like to watch a movie or play ball?" They gave you choices between safe options. Now that you are older, your parents are not always with you. You make many decisions on your own.

The question is, will you make wise decisions? That is why we are writing this book. We want you to make wise decisions—decisions that will give you a great life. As a young man, you need the wisdom of older adults. If you need to find your way through a city you've only lived in a short time, it would be foolish to think you could navigate it better than if you had someone who's lived there for years traveling alongside you. If you live with your father and mother, they can be your source of wisdom. They are not perfect, but they likely know more about life than you have yet discovered.

If you don't have a father in the home, how do you find a trusted man? We suggest that, first of all, you talk to your mother or grandmother. Perhaps they will know of someone they trust to be a positive role model for you. It may be your uncle, or your grandfather, or some other family member. The second place to find a responsible man is in the church. Many men who attend church regularly have made wise decisions in their own lives, and would be willing to help you make wise decisions in your life. Again, we suggest that you ask your mother to help you in finding a man in her family, or in the church. (A word to mothers who may be reading this: always have someone run a background check on anyone you are asking to mentor your son.) Another source is an organization called Big Brothers. This organization seeks to match responsible adult men with younger men who need a wise man in their lives.

If you read and discuss this book with your father, substitute father, or trusted adult, it will help you make wise decisions and thus give you a great life.

 I (Clarence) was fortunate enough to have a dad. In my early years, my father taught me the importance of hard work and being on time. He demonstrated how essential it is for a man to provide for his family, no matter the personal sacrifice to the dad. I learned how to treat a woman by watching how my dad treated my mom. He smiled when she called him "honeybun." He taught me commitment in marriage because he never left my mom. Mom constantly said, "Your dad is a good man." He must really have been because she never remarried after he died.

One of the things I remember my dad saying is, "No matter how rich or poor a man is, keeping his word tells you what kind of man he is." Dad was a man of few words. He never said to me, "I love you, son." I often wish I had heard those words. He seldom, if ever, commended me for my accomplishments. When I was fifteen years old I made the All-Star team at a Wake Forest University basketball camp and won a trophy for shooting the highest free-throw percentage in my age group and received a standing ovation from the other campers. Dad didn't say anything except, "Would you like a Coca-Cola?" I complained to Mom about Dad not loving me. She explained that Dad did love me, but *his* father never told him that he loved him. She said, "It is difficult for your dad to tell you something he never heard from his father." Mom continued, "Your father is so proud of you, but he doesn't know how to say it to you." Mom's words were like music to my ears, and I received them as truth. Even so, **I later promised myself that if I ever got married and had children, I would tell them that I love them often.** I now have three daughters, and I tell them every day that I love them. Dad wasn't perfect. Some of his habits I do not want to repeat, but I am forever grateful that he was my father. He died when I was twenty years old.

My Substitute Dad

When I was fourteen years old I met Gary Chapman. He worked as director of youth activities at a local church. My friend James and I went to a youth activity held in a gymnasium owned by the church. Gary initiated a relationship with me by coming onto the basketball court, which wasn't his comfort zone. But he wasn't coming to impress me with his basketball skills. He was coming to meet me. I began to attend the weekly youth meetings and listen to Gary teach. But what impressed me most was that he showed a personal interest in me. I felt that he genuinely cared about me and my life. He was the first person outside my immediate family who expressed personal interest in my life. I didn't know why, but I felt good having an adult male take an interest in me. I felt that I was the luckiest guy in the world because between the ages of fourteen and twenty I had two dads. After my dad died, Gary became my father figure. He's been like a father to me ever since.

Going to college required moving from North Carolina to Chicago, Illinois. Even with this tremendous distance between us, I knew I could always count on Gary. We kept in touch with each other, and he helped me with my college expenses. When I got married I asked him to be my best man. My daughters now consider him their grandfather, and he treats them as his grandchildren.

Now you know why I feel so strongly that every young man

should have a father or a trusted man in his life. **We need the wisdom of older men.**

I (Gary) was one of the fortunate ones in that I had a father and mother who were married to each other for sixty-two years. They loved each other, and they loved my sister and me. They took us to church every Sunday. They made sure that we had the opportunity to be involved in the youth activities during the week. My father not only attended church, but he sought to live by the teachings of Jesus. He believed that his role as a father was to love, support, and encourage his wife, and to love, support, and encourage his children. Beyond the family, he was active in the community, investing his time, energy, and money in the lives of other people. My dad taught me how to feed chickens, how to plant and cultivate a garden, how to mow grass, how to trim shrubs, and how to ride a bicycle.

Dad worked in a textile mill; they made towels, sheets, and pillowcases. The mill operated twenty-four hours a day. Some people went to work at 7 in the morning and finished at 3 in the afternoon. A second group of people went to work at 3 in the afternoon and finished at 11 p.m. A third group went to work at 11 p.m., working all night until 7 in the morning. My dad chose to work in the third group. He did this because he wanted to be at home every afternoon when we got out of school. So he worked all night, slept during the day, got up in the afternoon in order to be with us in the afternoon and evening. At the time I didn't recognize what a sacrifice that was. But looking back on it, I am deeply grateful that he chose to spend time with my sister and me.

When I got married and had a son and a daughter, I was working on a church staff, first as a youth leader, and later as a counselor. I guess you would not be surprised to know that I organized my schedule so that I would be home in the afternoon when my children arrived home, and spend those hours with them each day. I wish every young man had a father as devoted as that. However, **I'm fully aware that many young men do not have such a father.** That is why Clarence and I are so strong on the idea that every young man who does not have a father at home needs a strong man in his life. Another man may not be able to spend as much time with you as a father who lives in your house, but he can teach you skills, be there to watch you play sports or music, listen to you when you need to talk to someone, and help you make wise decisions. **It is not your fault that you do not have a father living with you. But it is your responsibility to talk to your mother, grandmother, or adult with whom you live and let them help you find a trustworthy man who can share his wisdom with you.**

What We Have Learned from Our Fathers and Other Wise Men

- ➤ Always do what you say you will do.
- ➤ Recognize every individual as important and worth your time and energy.
- ➤ Remember that life is not about fame or money. It is about using your abilities to help others.
- ➤ Love people even when they fail you.
- ➤ Put God first and seek to follow the teachings of Jesus.
- ➤ Don't feel sorry for yourself.
- ➤ Never forget that you are responsible for your decisions, and you must live with the consequences.
- ➤ Always tell the truth.

These are the kinds of things that a young man learns from a loving father, or another wise man. At the end of each chapter, we are giving you a list of questions you can ask yourself, to help you better understand each decision and its effect on your life. We want to encourage you to not only ask these questions of yourself, but also of your father, substitute father, or trusted adult. Remember that life isn't meant to be lived alone!

ASK YOURSELF...

1. How would you describe your relationship with your dad, if you have access to him? What do you appreciate about him?

2. What are some of the things you think you will do differently than your dad?

3. If your dad is an absentee dad, how do you feel about him, and why?

4. How would you describe your relationship with your mother?

5. What are some of the things you would like to learn from your father or another man?

6. What kind of father would you like to be?

CHOOSE TO SEEK KNOWLEDGE

THROUGH EDUCATION

Have you ever heard the old saying "Knowledge is power"? It's true. We are not talking about power to rule over other people, but power to help people. The true purpose of knowledge is to leave the world a better place than you found it. The more you learn, the greater impact your life will have. If you learn what to do when bitten by a poisonous snake, then you have the knowledge that may save the life of your friend when you are camping in the woods. Knowledge makes all the difference.

 In my home (Clarence), obtaining an education was not an option. It was the law, and my parents were the education police! They viewed education as a way for my older sister, Jean, and me to escape the poverty they felt we were experiencing as a family.

However, as a ten-year-old, school was not my idea of fun. I wanted to run, explore the woods behind my house, play ball—anything other than going to school. Sitting at a desk listening to a teacher was incredibly boring to me. Jean, who was a straight-A student, combined with my parents always comparing me to her, did not make my life any easier. They expected me to make all A's because Jean did. I didn't resent Jean, but I did resent always being compared to her. I wanted to be accepted on my own terms, so I began making some bad decisions, which I'll tell you about later.

Another ten-year-old who initially felt the same way I did about education is Dr. Ben Carson. He is now an internationally recognized neurosurgeon and serves our country as the Secretary of Housing and Urban Development. Dr. Carson remembers that in the fifth grade, his teacher and classmates would take it for granted that he would take a quiz without getting one question correct. He also had a bad temper, and often fought, even sometimes with his own mother. One Sunday while attending church he heard about a missionary medical doctor, and that became his dream. He wanted to learn how to help others. He wanted to be a medical doctor.

Dr. Carson's mother, who was a single parent, turned his life around. Due to his poor performance in school he had to pay the consequences for his decisions. His mother turned the TV off and began requiring him to read books and write reports on what he read. At first he resisted this, preferring to play with his friends. Then, he discovered that the books were taking him places his poverty would not allow him to go. So he began traveling the world through reading. One of his first books was *Up from Slavery,* an autobiography of Booker T. Washington who was born a slave and still learned how to read. Through knowledge he greatly enhanced the lives of thousands in his generation.

Dr. Ben Carson is also an African American. He reasoned that if Booker T Washington could do it, so could he. Suddenly reading became cool! Dr. Carson read about animals, science, mathematics, technology, music, and numerous other subjects. He graduated from high school with honors, went to Yale University, then medical school. At age thirty-two he became Director of Pediatric Neurosurgery at Johns Hopkins Center in Baltimore, Maryland. Dr. Carson has received the Presidential Medal of Freedom. He has written books and lectures sharing the story of his success. He says, "You have the possibility of controlling your own destiny, if you are willing to put in the appropriate amount of time and effort. And think big!" Dr. Carson also said, "God has given everyone at least one talent. Success is taking the talent(s) that God has given you and using all that to elevate other people." We think you would enjoy reading the story of his life in the book titled *Gifted Hands: The Ben Carson Story.*[1]

The foundational skill for gaining knowledge is learning to read. Dr. Carson's mother put him on the road to success by requiring him to read two books each week, and to give her the written report of what he had learned from those books. Since you are reading this book, we assume you know how to read. The question is, *are* you reading? **Are you filling your mind with knowledge by reading good books?** At the end of the chapter, we will suggest nine books we believe every young man should read before he reaches the age of eighteen.

We urge you above everything else to learn to read. Find the opportunities available in your school or your community where you can learn to read. Nothing is more crucial for your future than developing the ability to read.

 When my (Gary) sister Sandra and I were growing up, it never crossed our minds that we could drop out of high school. My father finished the eighth grade, and then left school to work on the farm. My mother dropped out of school in the eleventh grade to work in a textile mill to help support her family. However, they insisted that my sister and I would stay in school.

When I finished high school I had such a thirst for knowledge that I wanted to go to college. After finishing college I wanted my master's degree, and after the master's degree I had a vision of teaching on a college campus and knew that I needed the PhD degree. So, at the age of twenty-seven I finished my doctorate. I received my doctoral degree and have been teaching on and off the college campus for many years. My chosen field of interest has been marriage and family relationships, and that is what has motivated me to join with Clarence to write this book.

I believe that the deep desire of most young men is to someday grow up, be married, have children, and be a responsible husband and father. I believe that it is possible, and that the decisions you make between the ages of eleven and sixteen will profoundly affect your ability to reach that goal. **If you choose to make the wise decisions that we are focusing on in this book, you will be well on your way to a great life.**

 (Clarence) My educational journey was not as smooth as Gary's. While attending predominantly black schools with black teachers who nurtured me, I was a "B" student. But when integration forced me to attend a predominantly white school for my junior and senior high school years, with white teachers who didn't appear to be interested in me as a student, my grades dropped sharply. I almost didn't graduate from high school. I envisioned that my ticket to escaping poverty was basketball. I thought I had a "walk-on" basketball scholarship to a university, but the college coach got a coaching job in the NBA and left, and so did my walk-on scholarship.

However, amazingly, I did get accepted into a college. I did play basketball, but this college did not offer basketball scholarships. I must admit I was far more interested in basketball than in getting an education. At the end of the first semester of my senior year I flunked out of college. I went from being a star basketball player, part of the cool crowd, able to date any girl in school, having money, to being homeless and broke in less than a week. All because I refused to study and was not thinking carefully about my future. I made a stupid choice.

Knowing that my mom, now a single mother, could not afford to feed me, I didn't tell her that I had flunked out of school. In fact, I didn't tell anyone. I was so embarrassed. I don't know how Gary found out, but one day he called the apartment of my friend Johnny who gave me a bed to sleep in. Gary asked to talk to me, but I refused. Gary told Johnny that if I didn't talk to him, he would get on a plane and be there the next day. So I talked to Gary. He told me that he was disappointed, but he still believed in me, that this was not the end of the world, that we would come through this, and that I was not alone. It was great to know that someone still believed in me because I did not believe in myself.

I tried to get a job as a janitor at the college where I flunked out, but was turned down. My friend was moving out so I had to leave too, and was again briefly homeless. But Johnny helped me get a place to stay and work at the Chicago Gospel Youth Center where a man named CoCo, a Vietnam War veteran and now a janitor, gave me a mattress. I slept in an unused locker room.

Later, I accepted a basketball scholarship to another college and finished my bachelor's degree. With God's grace, and Gary's encouragement and help, I earned a master's degree and eventually received an honorary PhD. I have since invested my life trying to help others discover the meaning of life, and gain knowledge through education.

I believe that in life, we all get at least one chance for success. In most cases, there will be several chances for success, but we have to take advantage of those opportunities when they come. Staying in school and going to college are two of those opportunities within your grasp. I urge you to make the wise decision to seek knowledge through education.

Seeking to pursue a good education seems to be discouraged in some communities today, especially by young men. Some say, "Education is not the thing to do if you're going to be a *Man*. You need to be cool, be a part of the gang." However, the majority of people promoting this mindset often don't have a high-school education themselves. So they can't give an informed opinion. They're simply trying to hold others back and use them as puppets for their own purpose.

Want proof? What the gang doesn't appear to know is the following research. The Bureau of Labor and Statistics found the weekly earnings of a high school dropout (if they can get a job) is $554. Compare that with $726 for a high school graduate, and $1,310 for a college graduate.[2] Education seems to be, at the very least, an effective financial investment.

Also, according to the Bureau of Labor, graduates experience a considerably higher likelihood of gaining employment. The 2017 unemployment rate of people without a high school diploma was 7.7 percent compared to 5.3 percent of people who have a high school diploma; the unemployment rate for college graduates was 2.5 percent.[3]

The Northeastern University Center for Labor Market Studies released a report[4] showing that eighteen to thirty-four-year-old residents in Chicago without a diploma have more family and relationship struggles than those who graduate. This study also showed that dropouts face a much higher likelihood of going to jail than their graduated peers. Males have an especially high incarceration rate of 15 percent compared to 2 percent of female nongraduates. Lack of employment, income struggles, lack of access, and limited confidence are among factors contributing to higher rates of criminal activity among nongraduates.

So why do we drop all this knowledge about education, employment, and earnings in your ears? To make a sincere plea:

Thinking about Dropping Out? Don't!

Once you drop out of school, you will eventually discover that it is much worse being out of school. Initially it may be fun, but in a few weeks reality will set in, and you will begin experiencing limitations in your life due to your lack of education. Here are the reasons young men and women have given us for dropping out of school:

- ➤ I don't like school in general, or the school I am attending.
- ➤ I'm failing, getting bad grades, can't keep up with schoolwork.

➤ I couldn't get along with my teachers.

➤ I was suspended or expelled.

➤ I didn't feel safe at school.

➤ I got a job, and I couldn't handle school and work.

➤ I got married, or I got pregnant.

➤ I had a drug and alcohol problem.

We sympathize with young men who feel this way. But we believe that there are adults who would like to help you and work with you in solving these problems. We hope you have a father or another man you can talk about these things with, a man who can help you find the road to success. **It is not a sign of weakness to seek help. It is a sign of strength.** Don't try handling your situation by yourself, but try your best not to quit school.

In many ways staying in school is the choice of a lifetime. Struggling for a few years will be more than worth it to have career options later. If you, like me (Clarence), think that your ticket out of poverty is playing professional sports, let me remind you that the percentage of high school athletes who make it to the professional level is less than one percent. I say this not to discourage you, but to emphasize that the chances of your dreams becoming a reality are increased by attending college.

One obvious benefit of college is that you physically mature. When playing professional sports, you will be playing against grown men who are physically and mentally mature. Likewise, the more physically and mentally mature you are, the more likely you are to succeed. By not taking advantage of education, you may be unintentionally limiting your future life options for success and fulfillment. If you are not doing well in school, it does not mean that you can't, or it's too late. **It is never too late to do something good.** Achieving goals takes work. Don't deceive yourself by thinking that since you make bad grades now, you can't do better. There are teachers who care and tutors who can help, or even a fellow student who would be willing to help, if you are willing to ask.

 After flunking out of college, I (Clarence) attended night school in order to get my grades up. It was embarrassing, but I got my grades up and another college offered me a basketball scholarship. **There is no such thing as being too dumb to succeed—just too fearful, too lazy, or too proud.** Remember Dr. Ben Carson in the fifth grade? Dr. T. D. Jakes often says, **"You will win if you don't quit."** This is universally true about education and life. The decision to seek knowledge through education is yours to make. We hope you will be brave and choose this wise decision (and keep reading!).

ASK YOURSELF...

1. How do you feel about going to school, and why?

2. Are you struggling in school? What makes it hard for you?

3. How do you feel about asking the teacher or a fellow student for help? Why do you feel the way you do about getting academic assistance?

4. What are your parents' or other adults' attitude about you getting a quality education? What do your friends think about school?

5. Is it hard for you to study and do homework at home?

6. At this point in your life, do you have a dream of what you would like to accomplish? Where did this dream come from?

Take Action

➤ Consider watching one less TV show or playing one less game a night, or a week, and spend that time reading a book like Dr. Ben Carson did.

➤ Make sure you get daily physical exercise: walking, running, playing sports, etc.

➤ Work on managing your time: responsibilities at home, homework, practicing your sports, your activities online, and reading on your own.

➤ If you don't yet have a dream, continue to read about the lives of great men, and chances are your dream will come.

Suggested Books
We Think You Will Enjoy

Gifted Hands: The Ben Carson Story
By Cecil Murphey

Up from Slavery: An Autobiography
By Booker T. Washington

Winning the Race to Unity: Is Racial Reconciliation Really Working?
By Clarence Shuler

The Screwtape Letters
By C. S. Lewis

A Teen's Guide to the 5 Love Languages®: How to Understand Yourself and Improve All Your Relationships
By Gary Chapman and Paige Haley Drygas

Anger: Taming a Powerful Emotion
By Gary Chapman

How to Win Friends and Influence People
By Dale Carnegie

Martin Luther King Jr., On Leadership: Inspiration and Wisdom for Challenging Times
By Donald T. Phillips

The Case for Christ for Kids; *The Case for Christ for Students*
By Lee Strobel

Do Hard Things: A Teenage Rebellion Against Low Expectations
By Alex Harris

CHOOSE
TO MAKE
TECHNOLOGY
WORK
FOR YOU

If you have studied history, you know that there was a time in America when there were no cars, no highways, no airplanes, no phones, no electric lights in houses, no TV, and certainly no computers or smartphones. Think about what life must have been like! Yet in those days there were young men who made the wise decisions we have discussed in this book. On the other hand, there were young men who made bad decisions and wasted their lives in mindless activity and destructive behavior. In every generation there are young men who grow up to make the world a better place, and others who leave behind a trail of pain because of their poor decisions.

In this book we have challenged you to make wise decisions. In this chapter we will look at a challenge that those earlier generations never had to face—technology. It all began when Thomas Edison invented the light bulb. Later, he developed a system of electric power generation and distribution to homes, businesses, and factories—a crucial development in the modern industrial world. No more candles and oil lamps. Now every young man could read a book at night because a light bulb hung from the ceiling of his room.

Then Edison developed the phonograph on which music and lectures could be recorded and played back on a machine. Then came the motion picture.

Based upon this foundation we have seen a technological explosion. First there were silent movies and no color on the screen. All the scenes were black and white. Then came sound, then came color. Movie theatres flourished around the country. And then there was television. Before television families sat around the radio in the evening and listened to music or dramas. On Saturdays, I (Gary) would go to my uncle's house and watch TV because he was the only one in the community who had one. I know that is hard to imagine in today's world when virtually every house has a television. Nightly news programs gave us the ability to see and hear what was going on around the world while sitting in our living rooms. There were still no computers and no cellphones. That would come later.

Now the world is filled with computers, laptops, tablets, smartphones . . . With these new technological discoveries we can now spend every moment of every day watching sporting events, listening to music, watching movies, acquiring information, and sending and receiving messages from our friends, including photos and videos. Yes, it's a brave new world. Things are radically different for your generation. Chances are you can't remember a time before texting and social media. But this is your world, and in it you will make either wise or poor decisions. Our hope is that you will make wise decisions about technology—that you will control technology and not let it control you.

Through technology you have access to the world— both good and bad. You can spend your time entertaining yourself with sports, music, and video games. Or you can spend your time seeking to learn lessons from the past and dream dreams about how you can make the world a better place in the future. There is nothing wrong with sports, music, and video games. A little entertainment along the way is good for us. But if you become obsessed with these aspects of technology, you will miss out on the more important things in life.

In other countries around the world this obsession with entertainment has led to what is commonly called Internet Addiction Disorder. In China, Taiwan, and South Korea, as many as 30 percent of people may be addicted to the internet.[1] When young men are addicted to video games they cannot resist the urge to play, even if it disrupts their eating, sleeping, homework, and relating to family or friends. Our hope is that you will not fall into this type of addiction.

The human body and brain need time to relax; time for physical exercise, sleep, and talking with family and friends. Neurosurgeon Ben Carson, whom we met earlier in this book, once said, "Don't let anyone turn you into a slave. You are a slave if you let the media tell you that sports and entertainment are more important than developing your brain."[2] Your brain has millions of brain cells waiting to be nurtured and developed. You choose what to feed your brain.

Make the Most of Technology

So, how do you use technology to enrich your life, to equip you to reach your potential for good in the world? Hopefully, this is a question you can discuss with your mom or dad. However, we would like to make the following suggestions.

Use the internet to find information quickly. Do you want to know when Thomas Edison lived? Google his name and immediately you will find not only the years in which he lived but also his accomplishments. Would you like to know when the light bulb was invented, or the when the first computer was invented? Google the terms and you can find out immediately. Do you have questions about cars, trains, airplanes, or motorcycles? In an instant you can have all the information you desire on these topics from the internet. When we were your age, and were inquisitive about these matters, we had to go to the public library and look up these topics in the card catalog and find books that would answer our questions.

In today's world this information is available simply by pushing a few buttons or asking your smartphone with your voice. You live in an incredible world of instant information. Use technology to gain information on virtually any topic in which you have an interest. You can be the smartest person in your school simply by making use of the vast information available on the internet. How do bees make honey? How many of your friends can answer that question? You can learn it quickly on the internet.

Use the internet to help with your school homework assignments. Never be satisfied to simply read the assigned material or work the assigned math problem. Go online and try to learn something about the topic or math problem that was not assigned to you. **Go beyond what is expected.** Don't aspire to simply make a passing grade, aspire to be your best. This is far more profitable than simply consuming more entertainment on television or on your computer. Thomas Edison said, "If we did all the things we are capable of, we would literally astound ourselves."[3] During these years your brain is capable of processing more than you can imagine. Don't starve your brain. See your homework assignments not as a duty, not as a requirement, but as an adventure in learning.

Use the cellphone to stay in touch with your family and friends. The cellphone is normally the first step in entering the world of mobile phones. It is simply a portable telephone that can make and receive calls over a radio frequency link while the user is moving within a cellular service area. In the early stages of development there were no smartphones, only cellphones. Before the cellphone you could not make calls from an open field or on the sidewalk. You had to be inside the house talking on a phone that was linked to the telephone lines outside the house.

Cellphones were a huge step forward in communications. Your parents have probably already made the decision to give you a phone or not to give you a phone. Parents differ on the age at which they choose to give their children a phone. This is the decision of the parents because there is a monthly charge for using a cellphone, and most young people your age do not have an income that affords paying the monthly fees. Thus, you must honor your parents' decisions.

However, if your parents have given you a cellphone, you can utilize it to keep in touch. Tell them where you are and what's going on. If you get in trouble, use a cellphone to call your parents. When you have a cellphone your parents have peace of mind knowing that they are only a phone call away if you have a need.

Your parents can also call you on your cell. It is a sign of respect to answer your phone when they call, no matter what you are doing. They will not likely call you in the middle of your class at school, but they may call you after school hours when they wonder where you are and what you are doing, or they have something important to share with you. This ability to call and talk with parents wherever you are is a tremendous advantage in building strong and healthy relationships with your parents.

You may also call friends and other family members on your cellphone. It is a tool to be used to develop relationships with friends and family members.

Make the most of your smartphone. A smartphone is a mobile personal computer that can be held in your hand. On a smartphone you have the ability to place and receive voice or video calls, and create and receive text messages, have personal digital assistance, an event planner, media player, video games, GPS navigation, digital camera, and digital video camera. Essentially, the smartphone makes available to you all the functions of a computer. It is a huge step up from the cellphone. Again, parents differ regarding the age at which a young person is old enough to receive a smartphone. Again, we urge you to honor their decision. After all, they are the ones paying the monthly fees for the smartphone, and as parents they are responsible for doing what they think is best for you.

 If you have a smartphone, use it to send text messages and photos to your family and friends. When I (Gary) am traveling and see something that I think my grandchildren would enjoy, I take a photo and send it with a text message to my granddaughter, who is eighteen, and my grandson, who is sixteen. They always respond immediately. Though we are miles apart, we have touched each other and have communicated that we are thinking of each other. **Text messages are best used to send brief comments about**

nonemotional topics. It is not the best way to discuss an issue over which you have a conflict. This is best done in a face-to-face conversation.

Use a video call to talk to family members and friends when you would like to see them. This again is an amazing technology to use when family members are separated by distance. If you have an older brother or sister who is in college, you can talk to them and see them at the same time. The same is true for grandparents who are talking to and looking at grandchildren, carrying on a normal conversation. This technology serves a positive role in developing family relationships.

Use Facebook, Instagram, and other social media platforms to share photos and comments on subjects that are important to you. However, keep in mind that when you post something on social media it will be going to all of those with whom you are friends on that network. It is far different from sending a text message to one individual. Your social media friends may share what you have posted with their circle of friends. Thus, whatever you post on social media can ultimately go to thousands of people around the world. Therefore, be extremely careful about what you post on social media. If there is anyone in the world that you do not want to see what you are posting, then don't post it. Tweets, short or brief messages that you send to your Twitter network, also have the potential of going worldwide. Again, **be extremely careful about what you tweet.**

Don't tweet something that will hurt another individual or embarrass you. Even temporary, private posts on services like SnapChat, which promise to delete your post after the intended recipient views it, can be preserved and shared with others if the recipient takes a screen shot of your post with their phone. Once you send or share any word, image, or video, it's out of your hands. Be careful what you share!

In short, the positive use of technology is twofold. First is to enhance your knowledge of history, science, math, and the world around you. Second, to enhance relationships with family and friends. When technology is used for these two purposes it is extremely helpful. A third positive purpose of technology, if used in moderation, is for personal entertainment—music, sports, movies, games.

Use emails to ask questions that require longer answers, or to communicate information that is lengthy. It can be used to share with family members and friends something that is going on in your life that you want them to know. An email is essentially a letter that is communicated immediately and delivered without a postage stamp. In the days before computers we would handwrite letters, mail them, and they would be delivered three or four days later, expecting that perhaps in a week or two we would get a response. Email removes the time gap between when we send the information and when we get a response from the other person. It has greatly enhanced the process of communication.

The Dangers of Technology

It would be unkind if we did not warn you of the dangers if technology is misused. Here are some of the most common dangers.

Technology gives access to inaccurate and inappropriate information. Many things posted on the internet by individuals about various topics are simply not true. Anyone can say anything about any topic without giving any evidence that what they say is true. Therefore, don't assume that what you read posted by others on Facebook or other media sites is always true.

In addition to misinformation, there is also inappropriate information. The internet is filled with pornography and other sexually inappropriate websites. These websites can pop up when you are using the internet for totally wholesome purposes. And it is extremely easy to get diverted by these pop-ups and go to sites that will lead you into a destructive lifestyle. We will discuss this later in our chapter on pornography.

Cyberbullying has become a growing problem in the internet world, particularly among young men your age. Making negative and demeaning comments about (or aimed at) another person online is always inappropriate. My mother (Gary) taught me, "If you can't say something good about a person, then say nothing at all." That was good advice that I have sought to follow throughout my lifetime. How tragic that so many young men and women take pleasure in criticizing and saying negative things about others. We urge you not to participate in such activity. If someone bullies you on the internet, share it with your parents and let them help you process the issue.

Also, in a later chapter we will talk about the trend of *sexting*—sending inappropriate photos of yourself to someone else electronically. One additional thought on sexting: those who participate in sexting tend to encourage their friends to do the same, seeking to communicate the idea that "everyone's doing it." The fact is that *not* everyone is doing it, and those who are doing it will live to regret it. Many young girls have said, "I did it as a fun thing, but my boyfriend shared it with all of his friends, and now I'm totally embarrassed." We urge you never to ask a young girl to send you an inappropriate photo of herself. It is demeaning to her and does not speak well of you. On the other hand, never send a nude photo of yourself to anyone. Remember, it will lead to great embarrassment in the future. In some states, sexting is a felony.

Another danger in using the internet is that while you are searching for valuable information, you will often see other topics appear on the screen. It is easy to be distracted by these topics that appear. If you develop a habit of following those pop-ups you will be wasting time and diverting your attention from the purpose for which you went to the internet. **Focus on the information you are seeking to discover and don't follow a rabbit trail into five or six other topics.** The pull to distraction is a very real danger when using the internet.

Using electronic devices while you are doing other activities can be extremely dangerous—even life-threatening. Many states now have laws against texting and driving, or talking on your phone and driving. It can also be extremely dangerous using your smartphone while you walk down a flight of stairs, or walk across a busy road. Using your phone while carrying on a conversation with someone else is also extremely disrespectful to the other person. It communicates the message that whoever is texting or calling you is more important than the person you're actually with. This is not the way to build positive friendships.

Here's a sneaky danger we don't always think about: *thinking that I must respond immediately to every call, text, or email I receive.* It is this attitude that often leads us to interrupt a conversation with a friend to answer a phone call or text. One of the advantages of the smartphone is that the caller can leave a voicemail which you can respond to later. You can also respond to the text or email later. We must not allow technology to control our behavior. We must not allow phone calls, text messages, and emails to motivate us to an immediate response. That is abnormal and indicates that you are moving toward phone addiction.

Finally, we can become so addicted to our devices that we fail to build the skills necessary for developing positive human relationships. These skills involve listening to people talk with empathy. Empathy is trying to hear what they are saying and what they are feeling, so that we can know them more intimately and have a helpful response to them. It involves looking people in the eye when they are talking. It involves initiating conversations when we are around people. When we fail to develop these skills, we ultimately find ourselves isolated from other people. We are becoming a people tied to an electronic device, while we have few meaningful relationships with other people. In the adult world success is always tied to relationships. People who cannot develop positive, meaningful, face-to-face relationships in the workplace will often lose their job and end up going from one job to another throughout their lifetime. A rule to live by no matter how cool the technology: **people are always more important than devices.**

Earlier in the chapter we mentioned Internet Addiction Disorder. Unfortunately, this has become a common problem among young men and women in our culture. When a young man spends all his free time playing video games, watching YouTube videos, or searching the internet, and does not take time to read books, to get involved in recreation, to get proper sleep, and to build meaningful relationships, he forms a habit that will be hard to break when he gets older. The young man who is still playing video games with all his free time when he gets married will find a wife who will be extremely unhappy with his behavior. That is why we think this chapter is so important. Learning to control your use of electronic devices and not allowing them to control your life is an extremely important decision that will greatly impact your future. We urge you to make technology work for you, helping you reach your potential in gaining knowledge and insight that will help you enhance your life and the lives of others.

ASK YOURSELF...

1. What television shows do you like best? Why?

2. Keep a record of how many hours you watch television (including Netflix, etc.) this week. Do you feel like you watch too much TV? What about video games? What could you be doing that would be more meaningful?

If you have access to a computer, tablet, or laptop, how do you use it?

Homework ____
Getting information ____

Spending time on social media ____
Watching YouTube____

3. Do you have access to a smartphone? How do you use it?

4. Do you think you spend too much time using technology? Why?

5. Is your use of technology impacting how much you sleep?

6. If you have free time, what do you typically do?

7. Do you need to change your use of technology?

CHOOSE
TO BE
SUCCESSFUL:
WORK
HARD

What do successful people do? They *work* at it! And they work hard. No successful athlete got there by sitting on the couch watching TV or playing video games. Likely he played his sport in middle school (or earlier), high school, and college before he turned pro. Successful musicians spend hours practicing their instrument. Men and women who have successful businesses have spent years working hard. Nothing comes to the man who is idle.

You are never too young to learn how to work. In fact, if you don't learn to work during your teen years, you may never reach your potential.

If you are a teen or preteen, the most logical places for you to work are at home and at school. I hope your parents have given you certain responsibilities at home: keeping your room clean, washing dishes, cleaning the toilet, feeding the dog, taking out the trash, or other work assignments. If they have not, then I suggest you ask them, "What can I do that would make your life easier?"

At school the first place to work is in the classroom. Be enthusiastic when your teacher assigns a project. After school, do your homework before you watch TV or play video games. After working hard to complete all assignments, then you may find additional places to work at school: sports, drama, music, or other activities offered at your school. Whatever you do, work hard and do your best.

In the later teen years you may have a chance to work for money. Perhaps your parents will pay you for doing projects that are beyond your normal responsibilities. Perhaps you can mow grass or shovel snow for a neighbor who will pay you for helping them. The teen who looks for part-time jobs will usually find one.

In college many students work part-time for the university in order to help pay for their education. When you get to be an adult, if you get married, you will be responsible for working in order to support your wife and children.

The sooner you make the decision to be a hard worker, the more likely you are to become successful in life. Plan now to be a giver, not a taker. I will work hard so that I can give to those who are unable to work. Abraham Lincoln said, "You cannot build character and courage by taking away man's initiative and independence. You cannot help men permanently by doing for them what they could and should do for themselves."[1]

We hope you will decide now to take Abraham Lincoln's advice. If you cannot afford to go to the university, take courses at your local community college or trade school. Many offer online classes. Learn a skill and get a job, or join the military and support your country. Young men who feel good about themselves are young men who plan to work hard developing their skills making the world a better place.

 Unfortunately, I (Clarence) did not make this decision early enough. My mother said, "You're the laziest child I've ever seen." She was infuriated with me as she saw me trying to get out of working around the house. I would say, "I'm not lazy, I just don't like to work." She was right. I didn't like work of any kind.

Dad and Mom both grew up on farms where working wasn't optional. They developed a tremendous work ethic. It seemed Dad was always working two or three jobs to provide for us. Mom was a schoolteacher, but later she became a sales representative for Stanley Home Products.

I didn't inherit my parents' work ethic. All I ever wanted to do was have fun, be a great basketball player, and date girls. Work initially didn't enter the equation.

The Necessity of Work

Dad didn't give me options about working around the house. I had to mow our lawn every Saturday and daily wash and dry dishes with my sister (we didn't have a dishwasher). My parents even made me mow the yards of senior citizens.

Dad told me only once: "I'll take care of your basic needs, food, clothes for school and church, shoes and a roof over your head. Anything else you want, you'll have to work for it." No negotiating with Dad. I knew I wanted a leather basketball and new basketball shoes. So at fourteen, I began to work for Mom selling Stanley Home Products. This was one of the first direct sales companies where women would host parties for their friends to show them the cleaning and other household products they were selling that couldn't be bought in stores. I could make money quickly by hosting parties with the mothers of my buddies. So I worked until I could buy what I wanted, then quit. If I'd had more vision, it would have been smart to have kept working and put my earnings in a savings account.

I didn't work again until I went to college. Basketball scholarships weren't offered, but this college did provide free tuition. I needed a job to pay for room and board. I was hired as a janitor for $3.10 an hour, which was a lot of money in 1972. I worked thirty-four hours a week, slept about four hours nightly, with fifteen hours of classes, plus basketball practice.

A funny thing happened as I worked as a janitor; I began to take pride in my work and making things clean, even the urinals and toilets. I know it sounds crazy, but I felt good about myself.

There was a sense of satisfaction that came over me when

I did a good job, even as a janitor. And as I worked hard to make things as clean as possible, the time would begin to fly! Funny how that principle of satisfaction coming as a result of hard work still impacts me today. As I think about it, even mowing the yard the right way brought a sense of satisfaction. Of course, I never told my parents that!

Therefore, while in college I had to work to eat and have a place to sleep. My parents were too poor to financially help me go to college. In fact, they were never able to send me a dime. I was okay with that because they had cared for me all of my life. From my perspective, they didn't owe me anything. I also took pride in paying for my education myself.

Oops! I almost forgot about the girls!! A guy must have money to date girls. There were a few exceptions when the girls paid for the dates, but the majority of the time I paid.

At my second college I had a partial basketball scholarship my junior year and I didn't play my senior year, so I had to do what was termed a "work-study program." What was good about that was I learned skills, which I should, and would, have learned from Dad, had I not been so lazy.

Thus another benefit of working was learning various skills. **The more skills you learn, the more confident you become about yourself and life.** And for those of you who desire to marry, some women expect their husbands to have some basic knowledge of how to do little things around the house. Such knowledge provides security for wives and saves the family money.

Taking Studying Seriously

Academics—school—can be work as well. At college I didn't work hard academically. I thought I was being smart by not studying. That kind of thinking wasn't smart! Procrastinating with my assignments was one of my bad habits. But there were more than a few times that I wished I hadn't delayed doing my assignment until the last minute because I realized I enjoyed the assignment, and I was also enjoying learning.

When I got into graduate school I understood that I would need to work hard and not goof off. Again, I was fortunate that this graduate school offered financial assistance, but I also had to work again as a janitor. Gary Chapman got me a job working for Coca Cola as a vendor man. This meant I drove a van with supplies for vending machines and change machines. It was demanding work but provided incredible pay. Gary's idea was that if I did this work from January until it was time for me to go to graduate school, I wouldn't have to work during the school year. In another dumb move, I quit after two or three months.

But this time, in graduate school, I took studying seriously. Taking good readable notes was a priority for each class.

I got a single room, which reduced distractions. This isn't always possible in college or graduate school. After class and work, I created a study routine.

But even before college you will have big exams you'll need to study for. Often this will involve notes you have been taking (we hope!) during class. How can you remember all that information? Here are a few tips:

Read notes aloud—the more senses you use, the easier you learn. This way you see and hear the notes and it keeps your mind from wandering. It can cut your study time in half. Read the notes the first day seven times aloud.

Read your notes from the first day once, then the second day's notes seven times aloud. Then the third day. You get the idea.

The benefit is that you learn the material before each exam, eliminating cramming. And you'll remember the material long after the course is over.

This method helped me earn a 4.0 GPA my first semester with some of the toughest professors at the graduate school. I shared this method with several students struggling academically and their grades skyrocketed!

After years of not doing well academically, I felt so good to see that 4.0 GPA. I sent a copy of my grades to Gary. He wrote me saying, "I knew you could do it, but it is good seeing it in black and white." For me, there was a sense of satisfaction to be rewarded for studying so hard. Near the end of my time at graduate school, several professors encouraged me to enter the PhD program. Imagine that!

A similar feeling came from basketball success after practicing so hard for years. It is about self-worth, not self-worship.

Finding the Right Work

What is a great job? **A great job is one in which if you didn't get paid, you'd still want to do it.** Now, this doesn't mean that if you are in a boring job that you don't work hard, or give your best. You can still have satisfaction in your work even if no one else appreciates it.

As you are in school, think about what you'd like to do for the rest of your life—workwise.

My spirit seems to be that of an entrepreneur because I'm a risk taker and a rebel. And it is fun creating a market for what I want to do. Now, I help people with their relationships, and in turn, those people are teaching me about social media, creating my own videos, and editing them. This is exciting for me because I'm technologically challenged! But I love constant learning and the challenges of new adventures.

Writing books, which I've come to love, is something I

never thought I'd be doing, especially a guy who flunked out of college. I fell into writing. Gary asked me to write an article for women who were working at his church. Then a friend asked me to write an article about my relationship to Gary from a cross-cultural perspective. I was paid for that article. A president of a college saw that article and put it in a book he was writing. I'm not a bestselling author, but it is fun writing books that people say help them.

Now I make a living helping people through counseling, speaking at conferences, writing books, and tweeting.

But not too long ago, a client said, "You really seem to love what you do." I laughed to myself because what I'm doing is working. My amusement was triggered by my memory of mom's statement about me being so lazy. She's still right! What I do usually just seems like fun!

So, think about who you are and how you are wired. Then, think about the possibilities of making a living doing work that seems like fun. You'll be successful and, more importantly, you'll have satisfaction!

 My (Gary) earliest memories of "work" was digging up potatoes, picking tomatoes, and snapping green beans. My folks had a garden, and we raised much of what we ate. My dad was a hard worker. In my mind, I can still see him pushing the plow to soften the soil. In those years I learned that hard work pays off. There is no better food than that which comes straight from the garden.

In high school one summer I worked in a small local department store. I still remember putting together Easter baskets with plastic eggs and yellow rabbits. I worked mainly in the stockroom.

After my freshman year in college, I came home and worked in the local textile mill, working from 11:00 p.m. until 7:00 a.m. It was my first taste of really hard work.

In college I worked in a warehouse that shipped out orders. I worked from 3:00 p.m. until 7:00 p.m., then I would go back to my room and study until 11:00 p.m. One year I worked as a janitor at a middle school. All of those jobs made it possible for me to go to college. They also taught me the value of work.

At your age you don't need to know the kind of work you would like to do for the rest of your life. However, it's fun to dream. What would life be like if you were a pilot, a teacher, a doctor, a farmer, an athlete, an attorney, a janitor, a builder, a banker, or a businessman? Or, what about working for a tech company or driving a truck across the country, or being a park ranger, or scientist? The list is endless.

One way to explore the possibilities is to talk with men who are working and ask them to tell you what they like about their jobs, and what they find most difficult. If you find something that really seems exciting to you, then that man may even let you spend a day with him on the job in the summer when school is out.

Having dreams will give guidance in what you decide to study in college or trade school. Imagine a job that you think you would enjoy. Talk to someone who has that kind of job. Learn as much as you can about the kind of training you would need in order to get that kind of job.

Another consideration is, "How would I be able to help people if I had that job?" A meaningful job needs to be something you enjoy, something that serves others, and something that will pay you enough to support a family.

 I (Gary) for many years have worked as a counselor on the staff of a large church. I too have written many books and now speak all over the world. I really enjoy my work. Someone asked me, "What would you like to do if you retired?" I said, "I'd like to do what I'm doing."

Our hope for you is that someday you will invest your life in work that you love doing.

ASK YOURSELF...

1. Do you have regular responsibilities at home? What are they? Do you do this work with a positive attitude? Do you get paid for extra work you do at home? Do you ever work for neighbors who pay you for your work?

2. After reading this chapter, how does it make you feel about your study efforts in school? Do you have good or poor study habits? Don't forget to try out the study tips we suggested and see if they work for you.

3. When you imagine a job that you would like for a lifetime, what job comes to your mind? Do you know anyone who has that kind of job? Have you talked to that person about what kind of training you would need for that job?

4. Would you be willing to ask your parents, or some other trusted adult, to help you learn more about the kind of job that interests you?

5. Do you think you will be more successful in working for an organization, or running it? Why? (Nothing is wrong with either choice.)

6. Right now, where do you need to work harder and/ or more enthusiastically?

WISE DECISION #5

CHOOSE TO RESPECT GIRLS & WOMEN

Have you ever had to make that dreaded walk across the room, at a school function or party, from the safety of your boys to ask the girl you like for a dance? It usually goes something like this: She was hanging with her girls. Inevitably, one of her girlfriends spotted you coming. Then, they all turned inward toward each other, giggling as you approached. By then, it was too late to turn back because everyone else in the room was watching! You saw the girl with whom you wanted to dance. You tried not looking at her, but you couldn't help but stare at her all the more, as you got closer. All the girls knew exactly who you were going to ask. Again, they turned into a circle, laughing as they asked her, "Are you going to dance with him?" The tone of their question informed the girl of your dreams of their approval, rejection, or if she had options. Thus, her personal preference may be overriden by peer pressure. Such groups often determined if young men got that dance with that special girl.

Finally, you arrived. Walking across the room felt like it took two hours, but it was only seconds. You had to ask this girl for a dance in front of all of her friends and everybody else. If her answer was "yes," you earned cool points, cred, or *swag,* or whatever you want to call it. If her answer was "no," you lost the invisible points that we keep score with in our social groups, and risked not dancing the rest of the night, as everyone took their cues from this group's response to you. Even more difficult than asking this girl for a dance in front of her girls was the long walk back to your group if she turned you down.

Pursuing girls is something that most guys aren't very used to and that's why having a father or trusted adult in your life is so critical. A rejection experience like the one you just read could impact your future feelings about females; and whether to respect them or not. The opposite sex can be a great mystery and frustration that includes figuring out how to approach, get to know, and eventually love them and receive love in return.

Whether you realize it or not, asking a girl for a dance or a date takes courage, but it is also one of the highest forms of **respect** we can give to a young lady.

But **what else is involved in respecting women, and why should we?**

We both grew up in the South, where most fathers and other men taught boys, beginning at an early age, to be "gentlemen" with women—to open doors for females, to let them go first, to pull out chairs for them to sit, to walk on the sidewalk in between them and traffic, to give up our seat so a female could sit down. To say, "Yes, ma'am."

But is this "respect" for women?

Some women feel that such treatment is demeaning, not respectful. Others welcome it. But respect for women goes way beyond holding a door open (although manners are important!). It means seeing women—girls, your mom and grandma and aunts, sisters, friends—as equals. It means speaking politely to them. Respecting their opinions. Not interrupting. And most certainly, it means seeing them as more than just sexual beings or, worse, abusing them.

Even though women are about half the population in this country, we have a long tradition of treating them as second-class citizens. You might know that women couldn't even vote until 1920. (And yes, many other countries treat their women and girls much worse than they are treated in America.) While males are more accepting today of women as leaders in government, business, science and many other areas, we males still have a long way to go.

How entertainment portrays women

 Look at our entertainment. When it comes to rap music, I (Clarence) love some beats and others I don't, but the lyrics can be a deal breaker for me. In some rap music, the lyrics talk about females in degrading terms.

When girls or grown women hear these terms, it can't make them feel good about themselves. They can't feel good about or respect the males that use such terms. There is no escaping the fact that the music that we listen to can impact how we feel toward and treat women. You may need to reevaluate listening to any music that degrades women.

Some rap music and videos promote disrespecting females. Watching pornography is another way of demonstrating a lack of respect for women. We will talk more on this subject in the next chapter, but let's address this specific issue here: pornography is disrespectful to women because it treats the woman as an object to be observed, used, controlled, and disposed of when you are satisfied. In fact, one extreme manner in which women are treated in pornography is often male domination. Other times there is simulated rape. If any man says he respects women, yet still watches pornography, what he really means is, at best, he only respects women he knows personally. **We want you to be a man who respects all women in public and in private.**

Not to go unnoticed, many video games objectify women with unrealistic body proportions, skimpy clothing, and dumbed-down dialog. Even more disrespectful are those game franchises where most women encountered are prostitutes that can be picked up, shot, or run over with your stolen car.

With all these examples of discrimination in our history and the twisted media we consume, is it any wonder that so many men of all ages struggle with respecting women as equals in our schools, families, churches, social circles, and workplaces? Is it any wonder that we keep hearing stories of men accused of sexual assaults on women?

One additional area of media and entertainment worth mentioning here is sports.

Have you noticed that more and more college and professional athletes are being accused of, and some arrested for, domestic violence against their girlfriends or wives? Some of the highest-profile cases of violence against women are impacting the careers of athletes in the National Football League. One lost his career while he was still capable of playing at a productive level. His domestic violence incident cost him the respect of many women (and men) plus millions of dollars. In another case, a prized running back entered the season with a domestic violence charge. Even though he was never charged with a crime by the local police, the NFL did its own investigation and issued a six-game suspension.

One lesson here is plain: **our past actions can have future consequences.**

So what causes domestic violence? How can I learn to control my emotions and change my habits? Think about it.

If the college athletes and pro athletes grew up listening to and watching females consistently being disrespected, then this mistreatment of women becomes an acceptable norm. It's an important question for you to wrestle with: Would you say that domestic violence against women is linked to what men listen to and/or watch?

A real man controls his emotions and is not controlled by his emotions.

You, of course, are not a big-time athlete or hip-hop star (and we want to add that there are many outstanding men among these groups). Maybe you're just trying to figure out your relationships with young women. Maybe you haven't had great examples of how men treat women. But now is the time to start building a healthy, respectful attitude toward all women and girls.

Our heroes!

Think about it: without women, none of us males would be here. Think about your mother. Most of our mothers were or are amazing! They give birth to us, they nurse us, they bathe and take care of us when we are unable to care for ourselves. Most mothers are always protecting us, especially their sons! There is usually a special bond between mothers and sons, just like there can be between fathers and their daughters.

Most mothers teach us how to care for ourselves and they use their special "mom powers" to help us. They usually know who is going to be a good friend and who is bad news. They know the difference between a nice girl and one who is trouble. Most moms shower us with praise! Is this the kind of woman that deserves to be called ugly names? Of course not. Do you have sisters or aunts who love you? Do they deserve to be called ugly names? What about other females in your neighborhood or school who are just trying to figure out life, just like you? The sad truth is that we must be taught to respect others, and the media we consume and the heroes we worship are usually not going to teach us that.

Here is an example of a true hero: Do you have or know of a single mom who works two jobs in order to provide for her family? It is extremely difficult for a single mom, no matter how incredible, to fill in the role of a dad. The difficulty increases even further for a single mom raising a boy as he matures as a teenager. That's why we encourage young men living with a single mom to seek to find a trusted adult male to walk with him through life.

 As a teenager, I (Clarence) had great respect for females. My parents drove that into me. **It's been my experience that respecting girls actually makes you more attractive to them.** I believe that having respect for females prepared me for dating and eventually marriage. You see, if you like and want to love a woman, at any age, disrespecting her or other women around her actually works against you in a powerful way. When women feel disrespected, typically, it is difficult for them to find love, joy, or fulfillment in their relationship with the disrespectful person, and usually the relationship ends badly.

So for those of you who want a lifelong relationship with a wife, a critical step will be learning to respect females if you don't already.

ASK YOURSELF...

1. What are some ways you think girls/women are being disrespected by young and older men?

2. Do you feel that you respect females? If so, how do you demonstrate to a girl or a woman that you respect her? What can you do better?

3. Do you respect your mother and other females in your family? If "yes," why? How do you demonstrate this respect to them? Have you ever been disrespectful? What happened?

4. If you are being raised by a single mom, how do you show her respect? Do you help with work around your house or apartment? Do you take out the trash without being asked? Do you help clean the kitchen, so that is one less job your mom has to do?

5. Have the music you have listened to or have seen on videos influenced the way you view females? If "Yes," how? If "Yes," what do you need to do to begin respecting females? Are you brave enough or strong enough to stop listening to or watching something that promotes a lack of respect for women?

6. While men and women are clearly different, why do you think some men have a problem seeing women as equals? How can you be different while still respecting women?

7. If you were a father who had a daughter, how do you think you would feel if a boy or a man called her an ugly name? If you were her, how would that make you feel?

8. Consider asking your mother or sister (if you have one) or any female in your family to tell you if they have been disrespected and if so, how? How did their experiences make you feel? Why?

CHOOSE
TO BE
SEXUALLY
RESPONSIBLE

Liking girls is natural, normal, healthy, and appropriate for young men. But how we handle this attraction toward girls is exceedingly important. In college, I (Gary) studied anthropology, a study of various cultures around the world. All cultures have guidelines on how young men and young women are to relate to each other—what is appropriate and what is inappropriate. What has happened in American culture is that over the last sixty years we have abandoned the rules upon which our culture was built. We have promoted "sexual freedom," allowing young men and women to do almost anything sexually. However, what we were not told is the cost of such freedom. **We were not told that for every choice we make sexually, there are consequences.**

One hundred and ten million people in America have a sexually transmitted disease.[1] Hundreds of thousands of babies are aborted every year and never have the chance to live outside the womb. Many of these mothers and fathers live with deep regret. Hundreds of thousands of married men who practiced "sexual freedom" when they were single will also practice "sexual freedom" when they are married.

Many of these marriages will end in divorce, and the children of these marriages will live with broken hearts. These realities motivate us deeply to challenge you to make wise decisions related to sexuality. In this chapter we will challenge you to make three specific wise decisions that we are convinced, in the long term, will give you the greatest sense of sexual satisfaction. Both of us made these decisions, and now as adult men, we are extremely glad that we did so.

One last thing before we get to these three challenges: you are going to read some straightforward descriptions of your body, what you can do with your body, and some of the consequences you may experience if you don't accept these challenges as wise for your present and future. But because you can't undo many of these consequences, it's for that exact reason that we are writing so descriptively and directly; **we don't want you living with pain and regret.** So with this statement of sensitivity from both of us, let's look at the first challenge.

Challenge #1
I will not expose my body to sexually transmitted diseases.

Sexually transmitted infections occur when one has sexual intercourse or oral sex with someone who is already infected. Estimates suggest that young people fifteen to twenty-four years of age acquire nearly half of all sexually transmitted diseases each year.[2] There are hundreds of sexually transmitted infections. We will mention only a few of the most serious. Perhaps the best known is HIV, the virus that leads to AIDS.

HIV (Human Immunodeficiency Virus)

There are fifty-six thousand new cases of HIV every year. Twenty-five percent of these are young people ages eighteen to twenty-four. Most new HIV infections among youth occur among gay and bisexual males. Almost 60 percent of youth who have HIV do not know they are infected; therefore, when they become involved in sexual activity they are passing along the virus to others and don't even know they are doing it.[3]

Syphilis

Syphilis is an STD that can lead to serious issues if not treated. In the beginning stage, it may be noticed as a single sore. Because it's painless, the sore can easily be overlooked. The secondary stage will be evidenced by skin rashes, or sores in your mouth, or rough, red, or reddish brown spots on the palm of your hands, the bottoms of your feet, or on the back. The late stages produce difficulty coordinating muscle movements, numbness, blindness, and dementia. In the late stages the disease damages internal organs and can bring about death. The majority of early syphilis cases are currently found among men who have sex with men, but women and unborn children are also at risk of infection. Syphilis is curable with antibiotics. However, treatment may not reverse damage that the infection has already caused.[4] While the health problems caused by syphilis are serious in their own right, the genital sores caused by syphilis also make it easier to transmit and acquire HIV infection sexually.

Gonorrhea

Gonorrhea is a sexually transmitted disease that can affect both men and women. It can produce infections in the genitals, rectum, and throat. It is a very common STD among people ages fifteen to twenty-four. You can get gonorrhea by having sex with anyone who is infected. Some men who have gonorrhea might not have any symptoms. However, men who do have symptoms may have: a burning sensation when urinating; a white, yellow, or green discharge from the penis; painful or swollen testicles. Rectal infections may include: anal itching, soreness, bleeding, or painful bowel movements. If left untreated, gonorrhea can produce serious and lifelong problems in men and women. For men, gonorrhea can lead to a painful testicular condition and, in rare instances, cause sterility. In other rare instances, gonorrhea can spread to blood and joints if untreated, which can lead to death.[5]

Genital HPV Infection

Human papillomavirus (HPV) is the most prevalent STD in the United States. There are various types of HPV. Some types can produce health issues such as genital warts and cancers. As with all other sexually transmitted diseases, you can get HPV by having sexual intercourse or oral sex with someone who has the virus. HPV can be transmitted even if an infected person is without symptoms.[6]

Genital Herpes

Herpes is another common sexually transmitted disease. In the United States over one out of every six people ages fourteen to forty-nine have it. You can get herpes by having sexual intercourse or oral sex with someone who has the disease. Genital herpes sores usually appear as blisters on or near the genitals, rectum, or mouth. These blisters break and produce painful sores that may take weeks to heal. This is sometimes called "having an outbreak." The first outbreak someone has may be accompanied by flu-like symptoms (e.g., fever, aches, swollen glands). Herpes is incurable, but certain medicines can stop or limit outbreaks. Condoms may lower (but not eliminate) the risk of getting herpes. Sores or other herpes symptoms may heighten the risk of spreading herpes to others. But even if someone does not have herpes symptoms, they can still infect their partners.[7]

How Common Are STDs?

Sexually transmitted diseases are common, especially among young people. There are about twenty million new cases of sexually transmitted infections each year in the United States, and about half of these are in people between the ages of fifteen and twenty-four.[8] Some of these STDs described above, as well as others we have not noted, can be cured with the proper medication. Others can't be cured, but you can take medicine to help with the symptoms. STDs that are not treated can become extremely dangerous.

So how can you protect yourself from sexually transmitted diseases? According to the Centers for Disease Control and Prevention of the United States Government, "The surest way to protect yourself against STDs is to not have sex. That means not having any vaginal, anal, or oral sex (abstinence). . . . It is okay to say 'no' if you don't want to have sex."[9] We fully agree with this advice and are asking you to take the challenge of not exposing your body to sexually transmitted diseases. Some young men think that condoms will keep them from getting an infection. This is not true, since a condom does not cover all of the infected areas.

If you have questions about sexuality, we encourage you to talk to your parents or other trusted adults. Don't be afraid to ask honest questions. Remember, they were also once teenagers. If you want to learn more about the facts of sexually transmitted diseases, Google "Centers for Disease Control and Prevention." You will find numerous articles dealing with various sexually transmitted diseases.

CHALLENGE #2
I WILL HAVE SEX ONLY AFTER I GET MARRIED.

This challenge may seem similar to the first, not to allow your body to be exposed to sexually transmitted diseases. However, we have found that those young men who take the challenge not to have sexual intercourse, or oral sex, or any other intimate sexual relationship before they get married are far more likely to draw strong guidelines for all their dating relationships. They will not put themselves in situations where they are likely to compromise their wise decision to abstain from sexual intimacy before marriage.

We also encourage you to share with your dating partner your decision not to have sex until after you are married. Giving them this information will encourage them if they have made the same wise decision, and if they have not, your decision may help them reach a similar decision.

One of the reasons for waiting until marriage to have sexual intercourse is that most young men are not in a position to be responsible for paying for a child that was conceived out of wedlock. If a young man has sex with a girl and she becomes pregnant, it is his moral and legal responsibility to pay for that child until he/she becomes eighteen years of age, even if he doesn't marry the mother of the child. We think it is tragic when we hear certain athletes bragging about how many children they have fathered with different women. This is nothing but total irresponsibility.

Many young men think that if they use a condom there is no way that the young girl will get pregnant. All research indicates that condoms give no such guarantee. Talk to many married couples who have used condoms because they were not ready to have a child, and yet ended up with the wife becoming pregnant. The only way to assure yourself that you will not become a father before you get married is to make the decision to wait until marriage to have sexual intercourse.

Sex within marriage is a beautiful experience. You will never regret waiting until marriage. The purpose of sex within marriage is not just to produce babies, although that too is a wonderful experience. But sexual intercourse in marriage is a deeply bonding experience. It creates emotional intimacy. This is why almost all cultures throughout history have encouraged young men to wait until they are married to experience the joy of sexual intercourse. For those who follow the Christian faith, as we do, this is the standard that God laid down for all of those who seek to follow His teachings. It is the practice of abstinence before marriage, and full involvement after marriage that creates the most stable home environment in which to raise children.

So what are some other reasons for waiting until marriage to have sex other than avoiding STDs or paying child support? From my (Clarence's) marriage counseling experience, those who have sexual intercourse before marriage:

➤ Seldom marry the first person they have sex with.
➤ Lower their ability to be committed to a relationship with only one person.
➤ Experience less sexual satisfaction when they do marry.
➤ Have less sexual intercourse after marriage.
➤ Increase their chance of divorce.
➤ Find it hard to experience a closeness or intimacy in their relationships, thus, not experiencing satisfaction, but frustration.
➤ Often deeply regret doing so.
➤ Discover that even if you marry the young lady you sleep with, she often feels she can't really trust you and wonders if you will be faithful to her.

Sexual intimacy requires an emotional, intellectual, social, and spiritual connection. Meaningful sexual intercourse is a celebration of these connections in a marriage relationship.

When a child grows up with a model of a mother and father who love each other, support and encourage each other, and work together to make the world a better place, that child is likely to become a productive adult reaching his/her potential for good in the world. On the other hand, those children who grow up in a home where they have no father, or where mom and dad do not love or mutually encourage each other, will need to work harder to make good decisions. Some of you who read this book may be growing up in those less than ideal families, but you do not have to repeat the mistakes of your parents. If you choose to make the wise and brave decisions we are discussing in this book, you will have a great life and change the direction and health of your family tree for generations to come!

Pornography

Before modern technology, pornography was not the threat it is today. However, in your world it is hard to avoid exposure to pornographic images. So, what is pornography? The word is a combination of two words. Porn comes from the Greek word for harlot (*porne*). A harlot is one who sells her body for money—often against her will. Today we call them prostitutes. Men pay to have sexual intercourse with them. We still have people who engage in this practice.

The second word is "graphy" which comes from the Greek word *grapho*, which means "to write." So, the earliest form of pornography was written descriptions of sexual activity intended to stimulate erotic or sexual feelings in the person who is reading. We still have this form of pornography as seen in some romantic novels.

Since the invention of cameras and video devices pornography has become more visual. The person is not just reading, but is now seeing sexually explicit activity designed to stimulate sexual feelings in the viewer. This is the kind of pornography that is most common today. Pornography may be seen in movies, on television, on computers, and smartphones. It is readily available and that is why it has become such a problem in our society.

The people who allow themselves to be filmed in nude and provocative scenes are selling their bodies for money. Those who watch pornography are supporting them and a whole industry aimed at exploiting women and men.

Would you want your sister to sell her body so men could look at her nude? Would you want your mother to be a harlot? We believe your answer will be "No!" So, why would you want to look at someone else's sister or mother exposing their naked body for money?

Pornography reduces a woman to a sex object and not a person of worth to be respected. She becomes an image that men look at for their own pleasure with no concern for her as a person. Why are we urging you not to get involved in viewing pornography?

- ➤ Pornography stimulates sexual desires that may seem difficult to control.
- ➤ Pornography fills the mind with sexual images that are difficult to erase.
- ➤ Pornography gives you a distorted picture of sex.
- ➤ Pornography leads you to view all girls as sex objects and not as equal humans.
- ➤ Pornography may give you the idea that girls are simply here to give you pleasure.

➤ Pornography exalts sex as the most important thing in life.

➤ Pornography does not tell you that after viewing it, you often feel bad about yourself, resulting in shame and a poor self-image.

➤ Pornography does not tell you that it can become addictive and cause great problems when you get married. No wife wants her husband to be hooked on pornography.

Therefore, we urge you not to view pornography. Not only will your commitment help you to respect women, it will be easier to keep challenge #2 if you avoid pornography.

We've already talked about sexting—using electronic messaging, like email, texts, or other messaging apps, to send sexually explicit words, images, or videos to another individual that you are presumably intimate with (or want to be). And after reading the definition of the word pornography, you can probably see that **sexting is just pornography intended for one person instead of a wider audience.** But one of the dangers with sexting is it can quickly turn to pornography when the intended recipient decides to betray your trust and share it with others. Another big danger of sexting especially for someone under the age of eighteen is that, depending on the local and state laws of the two people participating, you may be committing or causing someone else to be committing a child pornography crime. When this happens, you or someone you claim to care about could become a convicted sex offender, labeled for life. So beware the dangers of sexting.

Some young men are giving up their smartphones and returning to using flip phones as one way for them to not be defeated by pornography. They have adopted a "Whatever it takes" attitude to live free of pornography.

CHALLENGE #3
I WILL NOT ALLOW ANOTHER MALE TO TOUCH MY GENITALS.

By genitals we mean your penis, testicles, or your buttocks. Unfortunately, there are adult men who prey upon teenage boys for their own sexual satisfaction. Sometimes these are men in your extended family: uncles, grandfathers, stepfathers, mom's boyfriend, or even a brother—people you already know. On the other hand, there are online predators who make contact with you through your email, messaging apps, or social media, and seek to become friends with you, and ask to meet you at a certain place at a certain time. Such invitations should never be accepted, but should be shared with your parents or other trusted adults. Sometimes such sexual abuse is perpetrated in an athletic setting by a coach, staff member, or fellow athlete. Fortunately, most coaches and those involved in athletic events for teenagers are upright, responsible men. **But if you ever feel that anyone is asking you to do something you don't want to do, say no, run away, and report it to your parents or**

some other responsible adult as soon as possible. This type of sexual abuse is all too common in our culture.

Sometimes teenagers are reluctant to report such activity to their parents or other trusted adults because they are fearful, but the courageous thing is to report such a person so that they can be stopped and not prey upon other young men as well.

You may also encounter young men your own age who will try to talk you into "exploring" each other's body. Their efforts to persuade you are for their own pleasure. This can be a form of bullying, and it has become for some gangs a new rite of passage or initiation. These are forms of sexual abuse. We challenge you to resist their efforts and report it so it doesn't happen to someone else, like a younger brother or cousin.

While this challenge is primarily about adult men preying on underage guys, do not be lured by or accept the "attaboys" from other guys/men surrounding sexual activity with adult women: these older women can be equally predatory and are damaging in similar, but different ways. This type of encounter is not a conquest or an accomplishment for you, but an injury to a future healthy relationship with a woman closer to your age. No matter what buddies or even unhealthy adult male influences in your life might tell you, becoming sexually active with an adult woman is equally abusive and needs to be resisted and reported to your parents and the police.

So in this chapter we have given you three challenges, which lead to being sexually responsible:

1. I will not expose my body to sexually transmitted diseases.

2. I will have sex only after I get married.

3. I will not allow another male to touch my genitals.

You have a choice to make. Having sex before marriage puts you at risk for contracting sexually transmitted diseases. If you are having sex before marriage, the odds are that the girl, or girls, you are having sex with are doing the same thing with other young men. Consequently, you have no idea who, or how many sexual partners they have had. Nor do you know if they have one or more sexually transmitted diseases. **Sex before marriage can be like playing Russian roulette with your health and possibly your life.** Is it really worth the risk?

Sex before marriage also puts you at risk for getting a young woman pregnant. Are you ready for the responsibilities should that happen? If you think that abortion would be an easy way out, let us remind you that you cannot force the young woman to get an abortion, and if she chooses to get an abortion, she may well live to regret that decision. Young men also struggle for years with that decision. We ask you, is it really worth the risk?

Not allowing other males to take advantage of you sexually may call for real courage, but resisting such efforts on the part of other males, and reporting whatever happened to your parents, or some other trusted adult, will save you untold emotional and sexual struggles and possibly save others as well. We hope you will choose to be brave and make the wise decision of being sexually responsible.

ASK YOURSELF...

1. Do you remember when you first became aware of your sexual attraction to girls? If you are not yet attracted, don't worry about it.

2. Have you talked with your parents, or another adult about sex? If not, what keeps you from doing so?

3. Why do you think that almost all cultures have clear rules about what is permissible and what is not permissible between single men and women? Why do you think that most religions discourage sex before marriage?

4. How successful have you been to this point in being sexually responsible? Be honest with your assessment.

5. If you have been sexually involved, or someone has tried to take advantage of you sexually, how did you respond? Have you reported it to a responsible adult?

6. What do you consider the best way to avoid getting sexually transmitted diseases?

7. How do you think pornography could hurt your relationship with your girlfriend, if you have one, or your future wife?

8. How do you think your girlfriend, if you have one, or future wife would respond if she discovered you were addicted to pornography?

9. How can you avoid pornography?

You have decisions to make. We hope you will choose bravely and wisely.

Actions to Consider

➤ Consider Googling "Centers for Disease Control and Prevention" online and reading about the various sexually transmitted diseases, and the suggestions that are made to avoid such diseases.

➤ Consider talking to your parents or a responsible adult about the whole area of sexuality. Remember, they once were teenagers, and they can help you.

➤ Consider asking your parent or a trusted adult to read this chapter with you and discuss it.

CHOOSE TO LIVE
LONGER & HAPPIER
PART A:
AVOID
DRUGS & ALCOHOL

Let's start this chapter with an undeniable truth: the use of alcohol and drugs has destroyed the lives of more young men than any other life choice. Between the ages of eleven and sixteen the human brain is going through an extremely important phase of development. Alcohol and drugs interrupt this normal mental development. Often these harmful effects on the brain leave invisible but impactful scars for a lifetime. The decisions made under the influence of alcohol and drugs may lead to prison or even death.

There is no debate that our culture has made alcohol and drug use popular. Movies, television, and celebrities have painted the picture that alcohol and drug use will enrich your life and is necessary if you want to be popular or escape reality. The reality is that drug rehabilitation centers are filled with young men and adults who followed this advice. They are trying desperately to break the chains of the addiction that has brought them tremendous pain.

 I (Gary) remember the day I decided to make the decision not to drink alcohol. My grandfather was an alcoholic. My family lived three houses from my grandfather, so I saw him often. He was a kind and gentle man when he was not drinking, but he could be critical and mean when he was under the influence of alcohol. On a regular basis he would walk from his house (he did not own a car) to the place where he joined his buddies to spend the evening drinking and telling stories. At the end of the evening he had to walk back home, but by this time, he was often drunk.

I remember the night I heard a knock at the door, and a gentleman I did not know said to my father, "Your dad is drunk and has fallen, and is lying by the curb on the street. You better go help him." My dad looked at me and said, "Put your coat on. I need your help." I walked with my dad not knowing what I would see. But when we arrived, there was my grandfather lying by the curb on the side of the street babbling meaningless words and speaking harshly to us when we arrived. My dad and I pulled him up, and walked him to his house, and put him to bed. I walked home with my dad, feeling sorry for my grandfather. That's the night I decided not to drink alcohol. I was twelve years old. My grandfather lived several years after that, but he was never able to break the pull of alcohol. When I think of him today, I still feel sadness. I've always been grateful that I made the wise decision.

 I (Clarence) had a very different experience. When I was fourteen, a prestigious college prep school came to our school to recruit students for high school. They selected the young men who

ranked one through seven in the eighth grade. Unfortunately, I ranked number nine. I was disappointed, and felt
rejected. The prep school was impressive, attractive, and
free because of the full scholarships they offered. I desperately wanted to go. My family was poor. It seemed like I was
always in trouble with my parents, so I was hoping for a new
adventure—living away from home. Somehow, I missed out.

When my friends who attended the prep school came home
for Christmas, I couldn't wait to hear all of their stories
about their new school. Physically I had never set foot on a
prep school campus. Mentally, I visited the prep school my
buddies attended through their stories.

We gathered at my friend's house for our reunion. The
prep school guys were "gods" in the eyes of all of us who
weren't in prep school. These "gods" who were still our
friends spoke of all the wealth of their school, three incredible meals daily in a beautiful cafeteria, classrooms, dorm
rooms, gyms, and tennis courts. We hung on their every
word! Their prep school was all male, but they spoke of
their sister prep school, the beautiful rich girls, and the fun
of their social events.

My Friends, Drugs, and Me

We were all excited to hear their stories, but what came
next I've never forgotten, even to this day! Unexpectedly,

they lowered their voices as they began telling us of their experiences with drugs. With eyes wide open, we listened. None of us who were rejected by the prep school had experimented with drugs because we knew if we got caught our parents would kill us! When we were in junior high the US Government committed to fighting what it called "The War on Drugs." The most effective anti-drug commercial of my day had this tag line, "Will drugs turn you on, or will they turn on you?" We non–prep school guys were pretty convinced by these commercials that drugs weren't the best way to go, but our longtime friends told us a different story.

As they began speaking about the drugs, their eyes lit up. As I listened, I was surprised at how accessible the drugs were, and that for them, the drugs were free with no threat of parental discipline. They said their other schoolmates were rich and bought drugs for them. As they continued, they spoke with excitement as they recalled their various drug experiences. They spoke of the drugs taking control of their mind and body. Then, one of them mentioned that while he was on LSD he remembered that the room began to "breathe." Other friends told of various mind-altering experiences. Then, our prep school friends offered us drugs for free.

Making a Life-Changing Choice

Most of my life up to this point, I was popular, a member of the cool crowd, but definitely not the leader of the group. I was more of a follower, but this day began a change in my life. I couldn't buy into taking a substance that would take control over my mind and body. When the moment of truth arrived, and it was my turn to take the drugs in front of me, I said, "Guys, you know you are my friends. I hope we can stay friends, but I'm not doing drugs." I soon left. The guys respected me, and I respected them. We remained friends. I left by myself, just the way I came. On my way home, I felt good about myself because I'd made the right choice, and I didn't violate my conscience. I started liking me more for who I was. My friends and I still did things together, but that day I started becoming my own man, a leader, not just a follower of guys I thought were cool. Actually, drugs made them sort of *uncool* to me. Something within me told me that even though I may not be viewed as cool, saying no to drugs was the right choice to make.

Another reason I said no to drugs was because I was trying to be a great basketball player. I couldn't afford to risk letting drugs derail my dreams of playing basketball in college.

Alcohol and Me

On the other hand, my choice not to drink alcohol was made in a different way. Two of my aunts drank alcohol. When I was ten, one of them gave me a sip of her beer. The bitter taste turned me off to beer. The other one gave me some of her liquor. The results were the same. So, for the next few years I never had the desire to drink alcohol.

When I turned sixteen, I was now playing basketball; girls and partying were definitely on my agenda. My dad knew that drinks were at the parties that I attended. So one day, he took me into the kitchen and said, "I know that at the parties you attend, alcohol is there, and I imagine drugs. If I catch you with drugs, I'll kill you! But if you drink, I'd rather you get drunk at home." He pulled out a bottle of alcohol and said, "Drink as much as you like." I couldn't bring myself to do it. **Somehow, in that moment, it killed my desire to drink alcohol,** and I made the wise decision not to mess up my mind with alcohol. After I made my decision not to drink, Dad removed all the alcohol from the house.

Gary: My decision to stay away from drugs is imprinted in my mind forever. It was a beautiful fall afternoon. I was playing basketball in the backyard with friends. Behind the area where we were playing there was a large field that was covered with summer growth. All of a sudden, we heard the roar of a motorcycle, and we looked up to see the motorcycle cross the road, and fly off into the field. We raced to the site of the accident, and realized that the rider was seriously injured. One of my friends ran back to his house and called for help. We tried to talk to the rider of the motorcycle, but he never stopped screaming long enough to hear what we were trying to say. Soon the paramedics arrived and carefully untangled him from the motorcycle, put him in the ambulance and drove off. I don't think I'll ever re-move that image from my mind. I felt so sorry for the young man and so helpless.

The following week, we found out that the young man was heavily drugged when he ran off the road. That's the night I promised myself that I would never try drugs. I don't know what happened to the young man, whether he lived or died. But I knew that I did not want to walk that road.

The Consequences of Using Alcohol and Drugs

As older men, we now look back at our friends who chose the popular route and got involved with alcohol and drugs in those teenage years. They may have appeared cool back in high school, but most of them are not cool now. Most tell us, "I wish I had not used drugs back then because I'm paying for it now!"

Clarence: Some of the guys who took drugs that night when we were at my friend's house did not fare well. Some became drug addicts. When I return to my hometown, it is sad

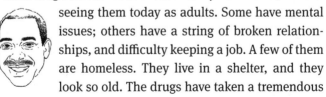

seeing them today as adults. Some have mental issues; others have a string of broken relation-ships, and difficulty keeping a job. A few of them are homeless. They live in a shelter, and they look so old. The drugs have taken a tremendous toll on their bodies. Not everyone who took drugs became addicted. Some went on on to hold responsible jobs and became productive citizens in the community. For them, I am grateful.

Some years ago, I became friends with the cook at a Tulsa tennis club. He was a recovering cocaine addict who had been clean for years. But something happened; he got depressed and then took cocaine again to try to escape his problem. He had a relapse. He lost his job, apartment, everything.

One of my neighbors was a recovering meth addict. When I met him, he had been clean for a year and ten months. He had a relapse, and he struggled daily with the pull of his addiction. Additionally, he struggled daily with the threat of losing his wife and children, and eventually did lose them. He recently died. His brother said, "He could never defeat his drug addiction." It is situations like these that make me glad that I made the wise decision not to mess up my mind with alcohol and drugs.

It's Your Choice: What Decision Will You Make?

 Years ago, I (Clarence) heard a counselor for the National Basketball Association (NBA) say to players who were entering their rookie season: "You will have choices, decisions, and consequences."

He continued, "The decisions you make will always have consequences. Are you willing to pay the consequences for some of your decisions?" It was a solemn reminder for me that my choices were extremely important.

We have never met an individual who regretted making the choice to refuse to mess up his brain with alcohol and drugs. But, we have each encountered hundreds of individuals who made the *popular* decision of trying drugs while they were young and have lived to regret that choice. So what about you? Will drugs and alcohol turn you on, or will they turn on you? Is it worth the risk?

ASK YOURSELF...

1. **Have you ever been offered drugs or alcohol? Did you accept or reject the offer? What led you to make the decision?**

2. **If you are using drugs and alcohol, why do you continue to do so? Do you have friends who are involved in drug and alcohol abuse? What can you learn from their choice?**

3. **Would real friends ask you to risk harming your brain or going to jail for the illegal use of drugs?**

4. Have your parents influenced you positively or negatively with regard to the use of drugs? What would you like to say to your parents?

5. Consider:

When you make the decision to refuse alcohol and drugs, you become a leader, and influence others in a positive direction.

Visit the following website for the facts about drugs and alcohol:

https://teens.drugabuse.gov/

CHOOSE TO LIVE

LONGER & HAPPIER

PART B:

AVOID

TOBACCO & MARIJUANA

When I (Clarence) was ten years old, my older sister, Jean, and I sneaked into my parents' bedroom and stole a cigarette from my dad's pack of Camels. I had already talked Jean into trying to smoke with me. We finally got the match lit. We were definitely rookies at this, as well as being nervous, hoping not to get caught!

Once the cigarette was lit we both inhaled a couple of times, which was immediately followed by a lot of coughing. Neither of us liked the taste of Dad's cigarettes. What motivated us to try smoking? I think we wanted to be like our dad. He worked for a tobacco company, and it seemed that most of the adults we knew smoked. Even on the TV reruns of old movies, all the actors and actresses smoked. It seemed to be the adult thing. I think we also wanted to see what we were missing because Mom and Dad had both told us we could not smoke.

During my high school years smoking was common for students. But the vast majority of the two thousand students at my school did not smoke. As an athlete, I was told not to smoke because smoking would make breathing more difficult. Our coaches believed that smoking would damage our lungs. Being an athlete and also being short, I was concerned that smoking might stunt my growth. I did not know if this was true or not, but I desperately wanted to be taller, so I couldn't afford to risk it.

For some, though it certainly was not true of everyone who smoked, smoking a cigarette was their first step to experimenting with drugs. In fact, some of my high school friends who smoked moved on to marijuana. I, on the other hand, decided not to smoke.

 Gary: My father also smoked cigarettes. In fact, it was his smoking that influenced me not to smoke. My dad not only worked in the local textile mill, but he also had a part-time business painting houses. When I was thirteen he taught me how to paint, and I worked with him on many of his projects. That was the year I decided not to smoke. My father had a continuous problem with coughing. The doctor told him that it was coming from smoking cigarettes. Yet, he continued to smoke. I remember one day as we were painting, he was at the top of a ladder when his coughing became so severe that he had to come down from the ladder. When his feet hit the ground his body was racked with deep, heavy coughs. When he finally regained his composure, I watched him reach into his pocket, and pull out his pack of cigarettes. He took both hands, and twisted the pack of cigarettes, destroying what remained. He threw them on the ground and said, "I'll never smoke another cigarette." Something inside of me became extremely proud of my father. That's the day I decided never to smoke cigarettes. I didn't want to go through all the physical problems I had watched my father encounter. From that day forward, he never smoked. When he had the desire to smoke, he would put a small breath mint in his mouth as a substitute, and he broke his addiction to tobacco.

Believe it or not, in those days, no one knew that tobacco caused cancer. While it was obvious that smoking brought on shortness of breath accompanied by hacking cough, no one realized that it was deadly. Just today, as I was driving to work listening to public radio, I heard a medical doctor make this statement. "The number one cancer-causing agent in this country is tobacco. We must find a way to help young people make the decision to avoid the use of tobacco." I did not hear the name of the doctor, but what he was saying is now common knowledge among those involved in cancer research.

Because of this knowledge, a link between cigarettes and cancer, in 2004, Hollywood began cutting back on smoking scenes in its movies. Why did Hollywood make this decision? It was their response to the following realities:

➤ 90% of smokers began smoking before the age of 21.
➤ Every day, almost 3,900 adolescents under 18 years of age try their first cigarette. More than 950 of them will become daily smokers.

➤ About 30 percent of teen smokers will continue smoking and die early from a smoking-related disease.

➤ Teen smokers are more likely to have panic attacks, anxiety disorders, and depression.

➤ 1 of 5 teenagers who are addicted to cigarettes will smoke 13–15 a day.

➤ Approximately 1.5 million packs of cigarettes are purchased for minors annually.

➤ Smoking can age skin faster, second only to the effect sun exposure has on giving premature wrinkles.

➤ On average, smokers die 13 to 14 years earlier than nonsmokers.

➤ According to the US Surgeon General, teenagers who smoke are three times more likely to use alcohol, eight times more likely to smoke marijuana, and 22 times more likely to use cocaine.

➤ The lungs of teens who smoke will not develop fully, which puts them at higher risk for lung disease.[1]

Why Not Get High?

Just like in the old days of smoking, many people say marijuana is harmless. They say marijuana just mellows you out—it just relaxes you. Marijuana, like any drug, controls you. You don't control it. This reality has always been our concern, and it's because of this fact we challenge you and other young men to make the wise decision and refuse to use marijuana.

Whenever you are making decisions, an essential principal is to look at the short-term and long-term effects of your choices. Make sure you see the big picture. Here are some well-established facts about marijuana use.[2]

Short-Term Effects

In low doses, marijuana produces:

• Poor memory and ability to learn

• Difficulty in thinking and solving problems

• Poor muscle coordination and judgment

• Short attention span

• Dangerous driving behavior

• Altered sense of time and space

• Food cravings

In larger doses, marijuana produces:

• Hallucinations

- Delusions

- Poor memory

- Not knowing where one is

- Anxiety attacks or feelings of paranoia

- Depression

Long-Term Effects

- Cancer. Marijuana contains the same cancer-causing chemicals found in tobacco smoke.

- Breathing problems. It creates the same kinds of breathing problems that cigarettes do: coughing and wheezing.

- Immune system. The THC in marijuana can damage the tissue and cells in the body that help protect against disease.

- Memory, learning, and energy are impaired.

- Fertility. Reproductive hormones are decreased. In men, there is less testosterone, causing decreased sperm counts and possible erectile dysfunction. In women, there may be irregular periods. Both problems would result in a decreased ability to conceive but not lead to complete infertility.

• Birth defects in unborn children.

(Source: www2.courtinfo.ca.gov/stopteendui/teens/resources/ substances/marijuana/short-and-long-term-effects.cfm)

For more information on these and other facts go to:

https://www.drugabuse.gov/publications/drugfacts/ marijuana

Let's also look at driving and marijuana. Smoking marijuana slows down your responses to sights and sounds, making you a dangerous driver. Marijuana makes you sleepy, distorts your sense of time and space, and lowers your ability to adapt to light and dark. It also lowers your ability to handle a quick series of tasks while driving. So a marijuana user's biggest driving problem is unexpected events, such as a car approaching from a side street or a child running into the street. This poor reaction time is worse when you are driving at night because marijuana causes a severe loss of night vision. Therefore, we are not only urging you to make the wise decision not to use marijuana, but we are cautioning you to never get in a car with someone who is under the influence of marijuana.

Some of you may be thinking since I (Clarence) live in one of the states where marijuana is legally sold, what's the problem? It is true that in those states you will not be breaking the law. But, unfortunately, just because something is legal does not mean it is beneficial. According to Bill Briggs, the Colorado Marijuana Study finds legal weed contains potent THC levels, which means that legal "Colorado marijuana is nearly twice as potent as illegal pot of past decades."[3] What does that mean? It means that you need to multiply the entire list of negative factors by two if you purchase and use legal marijuana.

Marijuana and Escapism

Some of you may feel that the pressures of life, such as a tough home life, or difficulties at school, or other personal problems give you a justifiable reason to use marijuana to escape your present circumstances. The problem with trying to escape by use of marijuana is that once you come down from being high, your problems are still there. In fact, you may have added to your problems because the drug is going to diminish your health. **The best way to deal with your personal problems is to reach out to parents or trusted adults, and let them help you find healthy ways to deal with those problems.**

Is the Use of Marijuana Worth Your Health?

 Both of us know many individuals who started smoking cigarettes when they were teens, moved on to marijuana, then to alcohol, and to other drugs. We have spent a great deal of our lives in the counseling office trying to help those individuals. We have seen how destructive this pathway can be. I (Clarence) have two personal friends who started using marijuana as teenagers. Both men are younger than me, but look much older. One man now speaks very slowly and has difficulty processing information. His memory has deteriorated drastically! Watching these two men over the years, and seeing countless others in jail or living on the streets, is all the incentive I need for me to say no to marijuana and other mind-altering drugs.

This Should Be an Easy Choice!

Whether you should use tobacco, marijuana, or any other kind of drug seems like a no-brainer to us. It just isn't worth it. Life can be difficult enough with our existing problems. There is no need to add to your problems by walking the road of drug use.

We are both adults who have enjoyed a loving marriage relationship and raising our children. I (Gary) am now also enjoying sharing life with my two grandchildren. We hate to think where both of us might have been had we chosen the road of drug use.

Three weeks ago I visited a man who was attached to an oxygen tank and had the plastic tubes in his nose in order to breathe. He was coughing periodically during our conversation when he said, "I wish I had never started smoking cigarettes when I was a teenager. I never went on to marijuana or other drugs, but tobacco alone has made my life difficult, and I know that I will soon die." I was deeply moved by his statement because I realized that had I made the same choice to smoke cigarettes as a teenager, I may now also be attached to an oxygen tank.

Now, you might be thinking, "What about vaping? You're not inhaling smoke but just water vapor?" Two things come to mind. First, e-cigarettes are still delivering the same drugs that their leafy cousins do. Second, they are *supposedly* less destructive to your lungs. Remember the history of cigarettes: of actors, advertisers, and even some doctors that thought they actually provided health *benefits*. The long-term effects of vaping are not known yet but the addictive properties of the active ingredients are not a mystery. Don't choose to be a lab rat for the vaping industry.

The time to think about your health is now. You only get one set of lungs, and they are supposed to last you a lifetime. They are like teeth. You have to take care of them now so they can take care of you later. The choice is yours. We hope you will be brave and make the wise decision of refusing to destroy your lungs with tobacco and marijuana.

We would like to encourage you to talk about this choice with your father, mother, or a trusted adult. You may want to discuss the following questions with them.

ASK YOURSELF...

1. **Have you ever smoked a cigarette? If so, how old were you when you did?**

2. **If you have smoked a cigarette or marijuana, how did it make you feel to be smoking? Did it make you feel older, tougher, more like what you think a man should be? Why do you think you need to smoke to feel that way?**

3. **Did you, or do you, smoke because of peer pressure? Do you think smoking to impress your friends is wise? If you need to smoke to impress them, are they really your friends?**

4. **If you are smoking, are you doing it legally? If you are breaking the law, how does this make you feel? If you are breaking the law, are you willing to pay the consequences?**

5. Whether you are smoking or not, have you thought about the short- and long-term effects of smoking cigarettes or marijuana on your health? Have you thought about the effects of marijuana on your driving (if you are old enough to drive)?

6. If you are old enough to drive, have you ever driven while high with your friends in the car with you? Can you imagine how you would feel if, while you were driving high, you had an accident and one of your friends died because you were high?

7. If you are an athlete, or want to be, how would you feel if your team lost a game because you were high? Do you think any of them would accept your excuse of being high?

If you need help to quit smoking cigarettes or marijuana, below are two free resources for more information:

https://therealcost.betobaccofree.hhs.gov/effects.html

and

http://smokefree.gov

CHOOSE TO BUILD DIVERSE FRIENDSHIPS

One of the realities of being human is that we are all different. Some are tall, some are short, some speak English and others Chinese or French, German, Spanish, or scores of other languages. Our skin color is often different. I (Gary) remember a song that I was taught as a child: "Red and yellow, black and white, they are precious in His sight, Jesus loves the little children of the world." I have always been grateful that my parents taught me that song. I think it was the belief that God loves all humans equally that made it easy for me to relate to people who had a different color of skin.

When I was a teenager the world was very different. African Americans went to one school. Whites went to another school. The same was true with the church. The same was true with the communities where we lived. And yet, because we were all humans we had a way of relating to each other as friends. My cousin, who lived next door, had a basketball hoop in his backyard. Every afternoon and on Saturdays young teenagers from the black community would come to our backyard and we joined in playing basketball. It was a fun time. It was one of the places where we could relate to each other as equals. I still have pleasant memories of those games because we played on teams together, not against each other. We were simply teenagers living in a world that we did not create, but we found a way to develop friendships across racial lines. We had no Native American, Latino, or Asian teenagers living anywhere near us, but I am sure if we had, they would have been invited to play with us.

I am encouraged that in today's world, which is very different from the world in which I grew up, all races go to school together. People can legally live in whatever community they desire, and all sports are open to blacks, whites, and other races. However, I am saddened that even though we have more opportunity to interface with those of different backgrounds, we often fail to develop friendships across racial lines.

All Equal in the Sight of God

Developing friendships with those of another race is not always easy. Sometimes you will be questioned by members of your own race as to why you are associating and being friendly with people who do not look like you. They may accuse you of abandoning your own race. This is especially true in America where we have a history of slavery, where for generations whites lorded it over blacks, which created huge resentment. I'm deeply grateful that long before I was born that chapter in American history came to an end, and the slaves were freed. I am saddened that so many people were (and still so often are) treated as second-class citizens. Many whites have had an attitude of superiority, and many blacks have had the feeling or experience of being persecuted. I am saddened even more that in today's culture we still often see resentment between blacks and whites. Because of this history, many blacks and whites are far more accepting of Asian, Hispanic, and Native American cultures than we are of each other.

I believe this can be changed if we can rediscover the reality that **we are all equal in the sight of God and treat each other as equals.** I believe that your generation has the potential of making this happen. In my opinion, it will not be done by political decisions, but it will happen when an individual of one race reaches out to become a friend to someone of another race.

 I (Clarence) believe there are many benefits of developing cross-cultural or racial friendships. One of those benefits is that we learn to see people as individuals, and not simply as Native, Asian, African, Hispanic, or Anglo-Americans. We realize that in every racial group each individual is important. Typically we build friendships with people we meet in the normal flow of life. As I mentioned earlier, when I was a teenager I loved basketball. I would walk four miles to sneak into Wake Forest University's gym to play against college students. I wanted to be the best, which only happens by playing against the best.

During one of those times I met Denny Hooks, son of Wake Forest's athletic director, Gene Hooks. Initially, I didn't like Denny. Not because he was white, but because he and I were so competitive. We often guarded each other. Denny was one of the best pure shooters I've ever seen. He and I developed a friendship because of our respect for each other's basketball abilities. We would talk after games, and he would invite me to his house to eat. In those days, we had an all-black YMCA basketball league. While civil rights laws had been passed, in reality much of our town was still segregated. Denny surprised me one day when he asked if he and some of his friends could join our black league. Reluctantly, I said yes, but I wondered how we would protect these white guys in the black part of town.

We actually won our first game. In our first game, Denny received a hard foul that the referees, who were also black, did not call. I was about to hit the player that hit him when Denny said to me, "Clarence, I've got to earn my respect in this league too! I can handle the physical play." At that point, he became my brother because of his toughness! Denny's being white wasn't an issue for me. He was a friend who shared a common interest in playing basketball.

In every racial group there are good people and bad people. This has nothing to do with the skin color, but has everything to do with their attitude. Those who choose to invest their lives in helping others will see people as individuals, and will seek to be friends regardless of their racial background. **Those who choose to focus on the negative things that have happened to them in life will feel that they must seek revenge.** They will do things that not only hurt others, but also will ultimately hurt themselves.

 I (Gary) remember the day that an older gentleman said to me, "Who is the black dude that you had in church with you today?" I replied, "He is not a black dude, he is Clarence." When we become friends, we do not focus on each other's racial identity, but we don't ignore it either. Rather we see them as a person who has great potential, and we choose to come alongside them, to be a friend who helps them achieve their potential.

The second value of building friendships with those who have a different background from you is that you learn much from each other. After my second year in college, I (Gary) worked as a counselor in a summer camp program for young African American students. I was the only white counselor in the entire camp. I had twelve young black guys in my cabin who I came to love dearly. They enriched my life and I like to think that I returned the favor. I will never forget the lesson I learned from one young man I'll call T. J. At the camp T. J. had decided that he wanted to be a follower of Jesus. We had taught the principles of honesty. We had talked about taking responsibility for our actions, and if we did something that was wrong, we should confess and seek to make restitution. T. J. said to me, "Four years ago I robbed a store. Now that I am following Jesus I feel like I have a responsibility to go acknowledge to the store owner what I did and take whatever punishment I deserve." I said, "You know that if you do this there is the possibility you may have to go to jail." He looked me straight in the eye and said, "I know, and I'm willing to do that. I want to take responsibility for my wrongdoing."

He asked me if I would go with him to confess his act of stealing. I had no car, so I said, "Let me talk with the director of the camp and see if he will give us a car, and if he will, I'll go with you." The director of the camp was a very wise man. He encouraged us to make the journey to the little town of Sweetwater, Tennessee. T. J. knew where the man lived who owned the store. He was a white man. We knocked on the front door together. When the man came to the door T. J. said, "You may remember four years ago when some things were stolen from your store. I was never caught, but I am the young man who stole those things from you. I have been to the Bible camp this summer, and I've become a follower of Jesus and I am trying to make right the wrongs in my life. So, I have come to confess and to do whatever I need to do to make things right."

The store owner looked at me and said, "And who are you?" I said, "I'm a counselor at the Bible camp, and I came with T. J. because he wanted to confess to you his wrongdoing." The man had been standing behind the screen door, but at this juncture he walked out on the porch. He took T. J. by the hand and looked him in the eye and said, "Young man, I too am a follower of Jesus, and I want to thank you for having the courage to come and confess to me your wrong-doing. And because you have confessed I want to forgive you, and I want to tell you that I am proud of you." They hugged each other and both of them cried, as did I. That's the day I learned how to confess my failures to those I had hurt, and also, how to forgive those who have wronged me. It was one of the most important lessons I've ever learned, and one that I hope you will learn as well.

 As I (Clarence) sit here writing this book, I realize how much I have learned from Gary Chapman. I told you earlier how we met at the gym of the church where he was working with young peo-ple. I was over at his house almost every Friday night, and would often be invited back on Saturdays. When I was twenty, my dad died. Gary became my second dad. He did the premarital counseling with Brenda and me. He was the best man at my wedding. (Shouldn't the groom be the "best man,"??) He is a grandfather to my daughters, and I consider his children as my younger sister and brother.

Respecting Differences

Another benefit of cross-racial friendships is that we learn to respect differences rather than condemn them. I (Clarence) will always remember the opportunity I had to go to Brazil and play against their Olympic basketball team. My Brazilian friends taught me enough Portuguese so that I could introduce myself, carry on a short conversation, and share how I came to know Christ. The Brazilians' faces would light up when I spoke their language, and my face would light up when I saw their hospitality.

While in Brazil, the relatives of those who taught me Portuguese had another player and me over for dinner. Everything was fine until they gave us salad. We had been told not to eat vegetables or salad that was not cooked. There were health concerns. Our Brazilian hosts began commenting in Portuguese saying, "They don't think our salad is clean." (I understood what they were saying.) My teammate and I were offending them in their home. I told my teammate that we needed to eat their salad, even if we got sick. He refused. I chose to eat their salad, and they smiled. And I didn't get sick. **Building friendships with people from other countries and different racial backgrounds enlarges one's world, giving you a deeper understanding for cultural differences.** Such experiences help you learn more about yourself.

Another observable difference is the way people speak the English language. We typically say people have different dialects. Some of these have to do with where people grew up. For instance, Southern dialect is very different from a New England dialect, even if the people have the same racial background. However, some of these differences are rooted in our racial backgrounds. A young man from India will speak the English language with a very different accent from a person who grew up in America. If you don't know the person you may think, "He has a strange accent." But if you become his friend you will likely say, "I like your ac-

cent." Racial background also affects our vocabulary. I (Gary) learned many new words when I began developing friendships with people across racial lines. It's always fascinating to develop one's vocabulary and learn new words.

Political views divide many people. People who come from different racial backgrounds many times have different political views. If you were raised in a Republican family you may wonder how anyone could ever be a Democrat. The same is true of those who were raised in a family who always voted Democrat. But when you become a friend, you can freely share with each other why you have the political views you have, and you can come to appreciate each other's perspective rather than arguing or condemning each other. **Friends may have different perspectives on many subjects, but they should not allow their differences to divide them.** Friends are committed to each other's well-being. They can discuss issues and share viewpoints, even disagree and still be committed to helping each other.

Friendships also expand one's experience. I (Gary) will never forget the first time I saw a piñata. I was in Honduras with a friend of mine. I found it fascinating to watch as people took sticks and beat the piñata hoping that the candy would fall out. Soon I was joining them in the excitement. It was a new experience for me, one that I will never forget, and still enjoy. When I was in Brazil I saw my first river houses, literally built on the river. The house rises and falls as the river rises and falls. I saw my first school boat, similar to a school bus, painted in the bright yellow color of a school bus that stopped at river houses to pick up the children and take them to school. It was a fascinating experience that I will always remember.

We have often discussed with each other whether or not race relations in America will get better. We cannot answer that question. But we do believe if it happens, it will happen one friendship at a time. We challenge you to make the wise decision of choosing to be brave and not judge people by the way they look. **Skin color and hair color are external.** We must never forget that all humans are created equal. We have differences to be sure, but our differences should never divide us; rather, they should enhance our lives.

ASK YOURSELF...

1. Have you felt that you were mistreated or ignored because you were different from others?

2. Do you have friends of a different culture? If so, how did that happen? What have you learned from your cross-cultural friend? Are you a better person because of this friendship? How?

3. Do you struggle with people who are different from you? If so, why? Why do you think people prejudge others?

4. Do you know a foreign language? Have you had the opportunity to speak your foreign language to a native of that language? If so, what was their response to you?

5. Have you ever sacrificed to help a friend or person of a different culture?

6. Will you accept our challenge to remember that all people are created equal? And will you refuse to discriminate because someone is different from you?

WISE DECISION #10

CHOOSE
TO INVEST
TIME IN
HELPING
OTHERS

All of us will spend our lives doing something. What we do will either make someone's life better—or bring them deep pain. Both of us have spent many hours listening to mothers crying over what their sons have done that landed them in prison. We have also listened to those sons share their own pain. One seventeen-year-old said, "I didn't mean to hurt anyone. I knew I shouldn't drink and drive, but I did, and now he is dead. I don't know how I can ever forgive myself." That young man did not intend to inflict pain on the lives of others, but he did. Everything we do has a positive or negative impact on others.

As humans, all of us are self-centered. In our minds the world revolves around us. That can be good if you care about yourself, about your body, and take care of yourself by exercising, eating right, getting enough sleep. But if you think *too* much about yourself, that can lead to selfishness. When we become selfish we are thinking only about what I can get out of life. That attitude may lead us to hurt others in an effort to make ourselves happy. The longer we live with that attitude, the more people we will hurt. Ultimately, we will regret what we have done.

The good news is we choose our attitude. We can choose selfishness, or we can choose to love and care for others. When we choose the attitude of love, we will look for ways to help others, and in so doing, we will find great satisfaction. Albert Schweitzer chose the attitude of love. He was a medical doctor who chose to invest his life, not in making money, but in going to Africa and helping thousands who had little access to medical help. Near the end of his life he was awarded the Nobel Peace Prize. Upon accepting the prize, he said this, "The only ones among you who will be really happy are those who will have sought and found how to serve."[1]

We agree fully with Albert Schweitzer. Both of us as marriage and family counselors have invested our lives in trying to help husbands and wives learn how to love each other, and love their children. We have invested hours listening to people express their deep pain over what others have done to them. Our objective is to help them rise above those painful experiences. Instead of seeking to make people suffer for what they've done, we challenge people to invest their lives in helping others. When we return evil for evil, when we hurt the people who have hurt us, we leave the world even darker. However, if we return good for evil we make the world a better place. We have both been to Africa and many other nations seeking to take the message of the power of love to change the world. Both of us have found that true happiness of which Dr. Schweitzer spoke. That is our desire for you.

You are young. You have the whole world ahead of you. The attitude you choose will determine how you invest your life. You can return hate for hate, or you can choose to love. **You can make decisions that hurt others, or you can make decisions that will help others.** That is why we are so hopeful that you will make the wise decision of investing your life in helping others.

 I (Clarence) must admit that serving others was a foreign concept to me until I was twenty years old, homeless, and without a source of income because of my selfishness, laziness, and pride. Remember I mentioned that I flunked out of college because of my arrogance in trying to beat the system.

My Failure—the Backdoor to My Success

Fortunately, a friend from college asked the Chicago Gospel Youth Center to hire me. The youth center was located in a section of Chicago where many homeless people lived. They were struggling with alcohol and drug addiction and had lost everything. The youth center was an old warehouse. Some businessmen had renovated it as a safe place for black youth who had nowhere to go. The leadership hired me for thirty dollars a week, which included a room in the locker room at the center. My job was to coach middle school and high school boys and girls in basketball and run the Awana program.

Discovering the Keys to Success in Life

My new position gave me authority over the kids. Yet, at the same time the kids easily related to me since I was young and good at basketball. Working with these kids opened my eyes to the tough life many of them experienced away from the center. For many, the center was a momentary sanctuary from real life. Approximately five hundred kids came weekly to the youth center. It was open Monday through Friday. It was a safe place: no bullying, fighting, or profanity was allowed. These kids, many from single-parent homes, were incredible, and so full of life! Most didn't have a defeated attitude.

Soon I began doing more than my job required. These boys and girls felt like my little brothers and sisters. They soaked up my love for them like sponges. As opportunities arose I taught them life lessons. For example, two fifteen-year-old young men from rival neighborhoods got into an argument that was about to turn violent. One was about to hit the other with a pool stick. I stepped between them. I sat both of them down to explain the big picture with fighting—that no one really wins long-term because whoever loses the fight usually wants revenge, and then these physical altercations escalate and too often someone will lose his life. Neither of them liked the idea of dying for a silly disagreement, so they became friends—wise choice! The young man who picked up the pool stick was suspended from the youth center for three days. He returned after his suspension a happier guy.

On Friday nights I would have the boys' team spend the night at the center and then drive them to the game on Saturday mornings. We would go to my favorite pizza place every Friday night. I didn't have much money, but I would buy pizza and sodas for all the guys. In order to have this experience the guys had to complete their life lessons before Friday evening.

All the twelve- to fourteen-year-old boys wanted to be on this team. The hardest thing I had to do was cutting guys from the team during tryouts. I was there for more than a year, and some who didn't make it the first year did so the second year. This was one of the life lessons I sought to teach: When things don't work out for you on your first try, don't quit. Thomas Edison sought to create the light bulb but it took over ten thousand tries before he saw the light. When asked about all that "failure" and why he never gave up he said, "I have not failed. I've just found 10,000 ways that won't work."[2] You must learn to work harder and smarter, if it is something you really want. For many of the youth, I became their big brother. I didn't have a younger brother, so these relationships became special to me, as well. I thought I was helping the kids, but in reality, they were also helping me. They were teaching me to be less selfish and to learn to care for others, especially those less fortunate than me. Though I was only making thirty dollars a week, I was incredibly wealthy in my relationships.

While I was working at the youth center another staffer who lived on the premises was a Vietnam War veteran. He was an amazing man, and could have worked anywhere, but he chose to work as a janitor at the center to help the kids. He also became an older brother to me. His humility and example of service was a life lesson for me.

Many years have passed since I worked at the youth center. I have had the pleasure of seeing some of these kids as adults. Many have become very successful in life, married with children, graduate degrees, pastors, college professors, media personalities and more. One of the twelve-year-olds I had cut from tryouts the first year, and who made the team the second year, is now a successful businessman. He also coaches boys' high school basketball, sending some to play in the Big Ten.

Some years later I was in a similar position in the Washington, DC area. There I worked with the poor and the wealthy. Some days I took the poor to Social Services, and other days I was in a three-piece suit sitting with politicians. In both settings I sought to help others.

 I (Gary) had the seeds of loving others planted in my mind as a child. I remember my mother preparing meals for others. I remember my father mowing the lawn of neighbors when the father of that home was in the hospital. I grew up in a church that emphasized the teachings of Jesus who said about Himself, "I did not come to be served, but to serve." Those who knew Jesus best said of Him, "He went about doing good." I have always been grateful for the emphasis of helping others that was a part of my teenage years.

Years later when I had children, I wanted them to learn the satisfaction of serving others. During the teen years I would take them with me to rake the leaves of elderly couples who were not able to do it themselves. I would knock on the door and say, "Hi, I am Gary Chapman, and I am trying to teach my children how to serve others. We would like to rake your leaves, if you would give us permission." The person would sometimes offer to pay us. I would say, "No. We don't want pay. We just want an opportunity to help you." They always expressed deep appreciation.

I would take my son on Saturday nights to the Juvenile Detention Center, and we would play Ping-Pong with teenagers there. They often expressed surprise that anyone would come and spend time with them. Now, as an older man, I find great satisfaction in watching my son and daughter investing their lives in helping others.

One of the joys we experience as counselors is helping people change their lives by removing destructive behavior patterns and learning the joy of serving others. When we see them investing their lives in helping others we know that the time we spent with them in counseling was truly worthwhile. Some people think that they have nothing to offer others, but all of us have certain knowledge and skills that can be used to help others.

When considering which adults and peers you look up to and allow to have great influence in your life, consider this question: **Does this person consistently serve others or only seek to serve himself?** When you use "service to others" as your guideline in choosing your mentors and best friends, then you can be sure that you will be positively coached and motivated to serve others and leave your world a better place than you found it because of your mentors.

Changing the World around You for the Better

We believe most people want to be loved, and we believe that most people respond positively when treated kindly. You can be a peacemaker and a difference-maker simply by seeking to serve others without hoping to get something in return. You can literally change your world by investing your life in helping others.

Helping others is like moving from the shooting guard position to a point guard position. While the shooting guard is focused primarily on scoring points, the point guard is supposed to be looking out for the welfare of the entire team, mentally and physically. Effective point guards put the success of the team before themselves. The satisfaction of helping others succeed is always more fulfilling than promoting yourself.

Practical Ways to Serve

One practical way to serve others would be helping a new student in your school find his or her way around school. Another option would be introducing this new student to your friends. Going to a new school can be unsettling enough on its own, and even harder with no friends.

Consider intentionally being nice to an unpopular kid at school. Maybe you can sit with him at lunch (or invite him to sit with you and your friends), walk down the hall together, include him when you hang out with your friends, or enlist one of your friends to also be kind.

Is there someone in the neighborhood, perhaps a senior citizen, you could help in some way? With yardwork or errands? While you're helping this senior citizen, don't be surprised by the life wisdom you might receive.

You could also serve your parent(s) at home by helping around the house. I realize that is a scary thought because your parent(s) may come to expect it, but think how your serving may surprise, please, and help someone you dearly love.

If you have siblings, you could even serve them. Of course, your siblings may pass out from the shock!

If you take a moment, you can probably think of many practical ways to serve others who intersect with your life.

Our culture often communicates that success is found in being rich and famous. But if that is your goal, be warned: **no amount of wealth and no level of fame will ever bring lasting satisfaction.** There's nothing wrong with making money, and nothing wrong if you happen to become famous. But these are not the things that bring life's greatest happiness. Happiness is truly found in serving others. If you do become wealthy, and/or famous, our challenge is that you will use your wealth and fame to help others.

ASK YOURSELF...

1. What do you think of this concept of serving others to find more meaning for your own life?

2. Do you ever struggle with being selfish? What would your parent(s) say? If you have siblings, what would they say? And why?

3. Can you think of a time when you served someone who could not repay you? If you did this, how did serving them make you feel?

4. Can you think of some people you can serve? Would you consider helping someone this week?

5. How do you think your school would be better if more people focused on serving others?

6. How do you think helping others would impact you?

CHOOSE
TO DISCOVER
THE TRUTH
ABOUT
GOD

Does it really matter what a person believes about God? We believe it matters supremely. There are many religions in the world, but they could not all be true for one simple reason: their beliefs often contradict each other. As humans we did not choose the country in which we would be born, nor did we choose our parents. Typically our parents teach us what they believe to be true about God. Because we trust our parents, we tend to believe what they say is true. However, in the teenage years when we are developing our abilities to think logically we begin to question if what we were taught is really true. Ultimately we will decide to believe what our parents have taught us, or we will choose to believe some other view about God.

Clarence and I (Gary) both had parents who took us to Christian churches each Sunday. We were taught the Christian view of God. We believed that God was the Creator of heaven and earth, that He also created plant life and animal life. But when it came to human beings, He created us male and female in His own image, which means that we are very different from the animals. We have the capacity to think, to reason, to make decisions, and to have a relationship with the God who created us. We were taught that

God had a purpose for each person's existence, and that He wants us to accomplish His purpose on earth and to spend eternity with Him after death in a place called heaven.

Jesus: "He Went About Doing Good"

However, growing up in a Christian home did not make us Christians. That was a decision we each had to make individually. Clarence made that decision at the age of sixteen. I made it a little earlier. Our decision was based primarily on the life and teachings of Jesus. No man in history has ever equaled the life and teachings of Jesus. A one-sentence summary of His life reads, "He went about doing good"[1] He healed the sick, He opened the eyes of the blind, He gave hearing to the deaf, and He raised the dead. He was more than a mere man, for no man could do the things He did. Though He was put to death by Roman soldiers, He said about His life, "No one takes it from me, but I lay it down of my own accord" (John 10:18). Those who murdered Him thought they were ending His life, but in reality, three days after being placed in the grave, He arose from the dead and appeared for over forty days to over five hundred people. To all who believed in Him he promised that they too would live beyond the grave.

We were both captivated by Jesus' life, His teachings, His death, and His resurrection. We became followers of Jesus. It was the wisest decision we have ever made. In studying

His life and teachings we have gained great wisdom, wisdom that has helped us make every decision we have ever made in life. Wisdom that has given us a purpose for living. Wisdom motivates us to continue to invest our lives in helping people.

We know that there are many religions in the world. This gives evidence to the reality that deep within the human heart and mind there is a belief that there is something beyond the physical world, something beyond what can be seen, and touched, and felt. Religion is man's attempt to find that supernatural world.

Most of the world's religions have one commonality. They have developed a system of what one must do in order to gain supernatural wisdom. Christianity is quite different. The Christian believes that God initiates a relationship with us rather than our seeking to find an unknown god. God, the Creator, reached out to us in the person of Jesus Christ, His Son. When we become followers of Christ we become children of God, and are assured the forgiveness of all our wrongdoing and the gift of eternal life with Him. It is true that we seek to follow the teachings of Jesus in our daily lifestyle, but it is not in order to be accepted by God. It is because we have been accepted by Him, and our deep desire is to please Him because we know that when following His teaching we will accomplish the greatest good with our lives.

In your teen years you will likely decide what you will believe about God that will greatly influence what kind of man you become. **We believe this will be the most important decision you will ever make.** It will profoundly affect all the other decisions you will make in life. Author and theologian A. W. Tozer once wrote, "What comes into our minds when we think about God is the most important thing about us."[2]

If you want to explore the Christian view of God, the easiest way is to get a Bible and read the four accounts of the life, teachings, death, and resurrection of Jesus. They are the New Testament books: Matthew, Mark, Luke, and John. If you wish to explore other world religions and how they compare to Christianity, which we believe is healthy, we recommend doing so with a parent or trusted friend. You may find an online overview of these religions at www .everystudent.com/features/connecting.html. What you come to believe about God is a personal decision that no one can force upon you, and we believe that it is the most important decision you will ever make.

Ask Yourself...

1. Do you believe it really matters what a person believes about God? Why?

2. What do your parents or parent believe about God? Would you be willing to talk with them about this?

3. Do you have a copy of the Bible? If not, would you ask your parent or someone you trust to get you a copy?

4. Would you be willing to read about the life and teachings of Jesus found in Matthew, Mark, Luke, and John in the Bible?

5. If you read these, make a list of the things Jesus taught us to do. Make another list of the things He taught us not to do.

6. The teachings of Jesus were given because He loves us and wants us to have a great life. Will you seek to follow His teachings?

CHOOSE LIFE
BY ASKING GOOD QUESTIONS

We have discussed eleven important decisions you will make as a young man. We have given you reasons why we believe these decisions are so important. **We want you to have a great life.** We want you to reach your potential for good in the world. These decisions are the foundation for a productive and meaningful life.

However, you will make hundreds of other decisions in the coming years. Decisions are a necessary part of life. You make scores of decisions every day. Some of these decisions are simple, such as "What clothes will I wear today?" Others will have much greater consequences, such as, "Will I get in the car if I know the driver is high on drugs?"

Therefore, we thought it would be helpful to give you a list of questions you can ask when faced with a difficult decision. Read these questions until they become a part of your normal thought process and we believe you will end up making brave and wise decisions.

- ➤ Will this have a negative or positive effect on my health?
- ➤ How will this impact my ability to think clearly?

➤ How will this decision impact my parents or other adults who care for me?

➤ Is this decision unlawful?

➤ Is this decision morally right or wrong?

➤ How will this decision impact my siblings?

➤ Am I being influenced by others to do something I really don't want to do?

➤ Will I stand up for what I know is right rather than give in to the pressure of others?

➤ How will this decision affect my future education?

➤ Is this decision consistent with what I believe about God?

➤ Will I be glad that I made this decision five years from now?

➤ Does this decision help me become the person I want to be?

Asking these questions will help you evaluate the consequences of your choices. Every decision has consequences, good or bad. We want you to have the benefit of making wise decisions.

There may be individuals who will seek to persuade you to do things that you know are unwise. We hope that you will have the courage to do what is right, good, and wholesome and not allow others to lead you down a negative path.

We hope you have had the benefit of reading this book with a parent or trusted adult. If so, we hope that you will turn to them when you need help in making a wise decision. Again, we remind you that the decisions you make now will largely determine the quality of life you will have as an adult.

We believe in you. We see you as a person of great value. We hope we will someday see some of the good things you will accomplish in life. We believe you can have a GREAT LIFE.

Acknowledgments

We are deeply grateful for our own parents who invested much effort in encouraging us to make wise decisions. We also appreciate our schoolteachers who challenged us to seek knowledge before making decisions.

As always the team at Northfield Publishing, Betsey Newenhuyse, Randall Payleitner, John Hinkley, and others helped sharpen our focus. Thanks to Michael DiMarco for his invaluable editorial assistance.

Notes

Introduction

1. Deborah Tannen, *The Argument Culture: Stopping America's War of Words* (New York: Ballantine Books, 1999).

Wise Decision #1:
Choose to Seek Wisdom from Parents or Trusted Adults

1. William Pollack, *Real Boys: Rescuing Our Sons from the Myths of Boyhood* (New York: Random House, 1998).

2. Read more at Roger Clegg, "Latest Statistics on Out-of-Wedlock Births," National Review, October 11, 2013, http://www.nationalreview.com/corner/360990/latest-statistics-out-wedlock-births-roger-clegg.

3. "Statistics," The Fatherless Generation, https://thefatherlessgeneration.wordpress.com/statistics/.

4. David Leonhardt, "A one-question quiz on the poverty trap," *New York Times*, October 4, 2018, https://www.nytimes.com/2018/10/04/opinion/child-poverty-family-income-neighborhood.html.

Wise Decision #2:
Choose to Seek Knowledge through Education

1. Ben Carson, *Gifted Hands: The Ben Carson Story* (Grand Rapids: Zondervan, 1996).

2. "Weekly earnings by educational attainment in second quarter 2018," Bureau of Labor Statistics, U.S. Department of Labor, *The Economics Daily*, July 20, 2018, https://www.bls.gov/opub/ted/2018/weekly-earnings-by-educational-attainment-in-second-quarter-2018.htm.

3. "Unemployment rate 2.5 percent for college grads, 7.7 percent for high school dropouts, January 2017," Bureau of Labor Statistics, U.S. Department of Labor, *The Economics Daily*, February 7, 2017, https://www.bls.gov/opub/ted/2017/unemployment-rate-2-point-5-percent-for-college-grads-7-point-7-percent-for-high-school-dropouts-january-2017.htm.

4. "High School Dropouts in Chicago and Illinois: The Growing Labor Market, Income, Civic, Social and Fiscal Costs of Dropping Out of High School," prepared by Andrew Sum et al., Center for Labor Market Studies, Northeastern University, November 2011, https://repository.library.northeastern.edu/downloads/neu:376384?datastream_id=content.

Wise Decision #3:
Choose to Make Technology Work for You

1. "FAQs," Net Addiction, netaddiction.com/faqs.

2. Ben Carson, BrainyQuote, https://www.brainyquote.com/quotes/ben_carson_490191.

3. Thomas Edison, quoted in Kevin Daum, "37 Quotes From Thomas Edison That Will Inspire Success," Inc., February 11, 2016, https://www.inc.com/kevin-daum/37-quotes-from-thomas-edison-that-will-bring-out-your-best.html.

Wise Decision #4:
Choose to Be Successful: Work Hard

1. Abraham Lincoln, quoted in Russ Crosson, *Your Life . . . Well Spent* (Eugene, OR: Harvest House Publishers, 2012), 149.

Wise Decision #6:
Choose to Be Sexually Responsible

1. Gail Bolan, "Foreword," "2016 Sexually Transmitted Diseases Surveillance," Centers for Disease Control and Prevention, last reviewed September 26, 2017, https://www.cdc.gov/std/stats16/foreword.htm.

2. "CDC Fact Sheet: Information for Teens and Young Adults: Staying Healthy and Preventing STDs," Centers for Disease Control and Prevention, last updated December 5, 2017, https://www.cdc.gov/std/life-stages-populations/stdfact-teens.htm.

3. "HIV Among Youth in the US," Centers for Disease Control and Prevention, November 2012, last updated

January 8, 2013, https://www.cdc.gov/vitalsigns/hiv amongyouth/index.html.

4. "Syphilis - CDC Fact Sheet," Centers for Disease Control and Prevention, last updated June 13, 2017, https://www.cdc.gov/std/syphilis/stdfact-syphilis.htm

5. "Gonorrhea - CDC Fact Sheet," Centers for Disease Control and Prevention, last updated October 4, 2017, https://www.cdc.gov/std/gonorrhea/stdfact-gonorrhea.htm.

6. "Genital HPV Infection - Fact Sheet," Centers for Disease Control and Prevention, last updated November 16, 2017, https://www.cdc.gov/std/hpv/stdfact-hpv.htm.

7. "Genital Herpes - CDC Fact Sheet," Centers for Disease Control and Prevention, last updated September 1, 2017, https://www.cdc.gov/std/herpes/stdfact-herpes.htm.

8. "Adolescents and Young Adults," Centers for Disease Control and Prevention, last updated December 8, 2017, https://www.cdc.gov/std/life-stages-populations/adolescents-youngadults.htm.

9. "CDC Fact Sheet: Information for Teens and Young Adults: Staying Healthy and Preventing STDs," Centers for Disease Control and Prevention, last updated December 5, 2017, https://www.cdc.gov/std/life-stages-populations/stdfact-teens.htm.

Wise Decision #8:
Choose to Live Longer and Happier: Part B: Avoid Tobacco and Marijuana

1. "Important facts on teen smoking," Step Up of St. Louis, https://www.stepupstl.org/resources.

2. "Short and Long Term Effects," www2.courtinfo.ca.gov/stopteendui/teens/resources/substances/marijuana/short-and-long-term-effects.cfm.

3. Bill Briggs, "Colorado Marijuana Study Finds Legal Weed Contains Potent THC Levels," CNBC, March 23, 2015, https://www.cnbc.com/2015/03/23/colorado-marijuana-study-finds-legal-weed-contains-potent-thc-levels.html.

Wise Decision #10:
Choose to Invest Time in Helping Others

1. Albert Schweitzer, *BrainyQuote*, https://www.brainyquote.com/quotes/albert_schweitzer_387027.

2. Thomas Edison, *BrainyQuote*, https://www.brainyquote.com/quotes/thomas_a_edison_132683.

Wise Decision #11:
Choose to Discover the Truth about God

1. Acts 10:38.

2. A. W. Tozer, *The Knowledge of the Holy* (New York: Harper Collins, 1978), 1.

About the Authors

Gary Chapman—author, speaker, and counselor—has a passion for helping young men reach their potential. He is the bestselling author of The 5 Love Languages series and the director of Marriage and Family Life Consultants, Inc. Gary travels the world presenting seminars, and his radio programs air on more than 400 stations. For more information, visit 5lovelanguages.com.

Clarence Shuler—As president of Building Lasting Relationships, Clarence interacts internationally with young men and women about friendships, dating, and sexuality. He speaks for Iron Sharpens Iron and in National Football League chapels. He's a member of Family Life's Marriage Conference Speaker Team. Clarence is a cross-cultural consultant for churches, corporations, and the military. For more information, visit www.clarenceshuler.com.

THE SECRET TO GREAT
RELATIONSHIPS—JUST FOR TEENS

IS RACIAL RECONCILIATION REALLY WORKING?

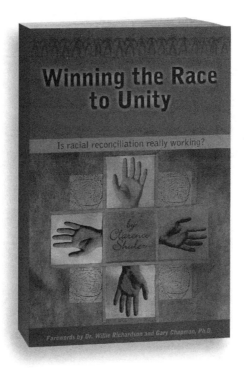

I WILL CHOOSE GREATNESS.

#CHOOSEGREATNESS

I WILL...

SEEK WISDOM FROM PARENTS
OR TRUSTED ADULTS

SEEK KNOWLEDGE THROUGH
EDUCATION

MAKE TECHNOLOGY WORK
FOR ME

CHOOSE TO BE SUCCESSFUL:
WORK HARD

RESPECT GIRLS/WOMEN

BE SEXUALLY RESPONSIBLE

LIVE LONGER AND HAPPIER

BUILD DIVERSE FRIENDSHIPS

INVEST TIME IN HELPING OTHERS

DISCOVER THE TRUTH
ABOUT GOD